AN
AUTOBIOGR
OF
TRAUMA

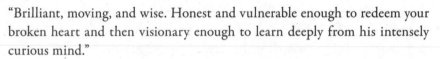

"Brilliant, moving, and wise. Honest and vulnerable enough to redeem your broken heart and then visionary enough to learn deeply from his intensely curious mind."

JACK KORNFIELD, AUTHOR OF *A PATH WITH HEART*

"This book is a peek behind the curtain of one of the greatest leaders of our time in the fields of spirituality and psychology. *An Autobiography of Trauma* is a powerfully transparent, knowledge-drenched, and generous invitation into the personal world of a man who birthed one of the most impactful models of trauma healing of all time. I felt giddy beholding his story of emergence, persistence, resilience, and leadership. This book moved me to apply Peter's awareness and perception to my own ongoing and deepening personal practice of returning to wholeness. Peter's work fosters healing, cohesion, and a 'coming home' to who we were each born to be."

ALANIS MORISSETTE, ARTIST, ACTIVIST, AND WHOLENESS ADVOCATE

"A valedictory ode to humanity penned by one of the seminal trauma pioneers and master healers of the past half century, this book is the account of a remarkable soul journey from searing pain to joy, from self-hatred to self-love. Its every page is infused with poetic eloquence, dramatic story-telling, unsparing honesty, and touching vulnerability. Prepare to be enchanted and to be instructed and, above all, prepare to be moved."

GABOR MATÉ, M.D., *NEW YORK TIMES* BESTSELLING AUTHOR OF *THE MYTH OF NORMAL: TRAUMA, ILLNESS AND HEALING IN A TOXIC CULTURE*

"A brave, self-revealing memoir of a man and his journey into wholeness. Levine intimately recounts the traumas and experiences that helped shape his legacy."

MARK WOLYNN, AUTHOR OF *IT DIDN'T START WITH YOU*

"This intimate and authentic memoir by Peter Levine, the developer of Somatic Experiencing, may serve as inspiration for all of us in our healing journeys."

ESTHER PEREL, *NEW YORK TIMES* BESTSELLING
AUTHOR OF *THE STATE OF AFFAIRS*

"I was so deeply touched by Peter Levine's story of facing severe violence and trauma as a child and how he transformed these wounds, restoring psyche, body, and soul. I am moved by his grace and authenticity in how he used his own deep wounding to help countless people around the world to heal from their wounds. After the first page, I could not put the book down as I accompanied him, as Chiron the wounded healer, on his healing journey. What I also found fascinating was his 'conversations' with Albert Einstein as an inner 'spirit guide,' a virtual mentor on his quest for knowledge, wisdom, wholeness, and connection."

DR. EDITH EVA EGER, *NEW YORK TIMES* BESTSELLING AUTHOR
OF *THE CHOICE: EMBRACE THE POSSIBLE* AND
THE GIFT: 14 LESSONS TO SAVE YOUR LIFE

"Peter Levine's vulnerable sharing of his own attachment and bodily assaults to well-being in this painful yet illuminating set of reflections reveals the inner workings of his psyche—soul, spirit, and mind—and a glimpse of the impact of both the inner and outer mentors that have guided him during various life stages. The raw human realities offered to us here may be triggering for some, yet they may also serve as an example of intellectual inspiration and courage. In these pages we see a journey to challenge dogma, to be open to the limitations of empirical linear science, and to see the liberations of a systems view of emergence and the importance of the body in healing. It is this openness to being a conduit of life's truths that can empower us all to embrace the fullness of life even in its most difficult moments."

DANIEL J. SIEGEL, M.D., *NEW YORK TIMES*
BESTSELLING AUTHOR OF *AWARE*

"This book is a powerful vehicle for a heroic narrative. True to the title, *An Autobiography of Trauma*, Levine provides the reader with an unfiltered glimpse into his personal traumas and his journey of healing. As the preeminent trauma therapist, it may not be surprising that his life was greatly influenced by adversity. Clearly his passion to reduce the burden of pain and suffering in others, and especially the consequences of childhood adversity, finds root in his own history. However, as Peter tells his story, we are privileged to see how he heroically repurposed the insights he gained through his own experiences to go well beyond a journey of self-healing to develop treatment models that are literally changing the world through their powerful positive impact on humanity. In this book we get to meet the bold, intuitive visionary who courageously convinced the mental health community of the important role that the body plays in experiencing the impact of trauma, both in expression and in serving as a welcoming, but often reluctant, partner in a journey of healing."

STEPHEN W. PORGES, PH.D., ORIGINATOR OF THE POLYVAGAL THEORY
AND AUTHOR OF *THE POCKET GUIDE TO THE POLYVAGAL THEORY*

"Peter Levine's autobiography explores the depths of his untold trauma story. The vulnerability he shares will help readers understand why he took the path toward being an accomplished healer. I believe his new book will inspire others to share their stories and find a place of wholeness."

DIANE POOLE HELLER, PH.D., AUTHOR OF
THE POWER OF ATTACHMENT

"A kaleidoscopic personal quest for sexual healing. *An Autobiography of Trauma* is beautifully written with smooth transitions between a myriad of shifting facets. At times this book is heartbreakingly painful and personal. It's also highly scientific, informative, and intellectual, highlighting the influence of Eros in letting go and ecstatic expansion while maintaining conscious awareness. Brilliant, breathtaking, and masterful.

DIANA RICHARDSON, AUTHOR OF *TANTRIC SEX
FOR LOVERS*, A 3-VOLUME BOXED SET

"We always want to know who the man or woman is behind the model, but too often their memoirs are promo pieces. In contrast, in this remarkable book, Peter Levine courageously reveals his own severe childhood trauma history, his consequent struggles to find intimacy, and how much connecting to the divine influenced his work and life. Somatic Experiencing is a powerful approach to healing trauma, and I'm so glad Peter is sharing the fascinating backstory to its development and to his healing journey. I was particularly touched by the chapters on sexuality and expect they will help people be more honest and open with themselves and others about this delicate and tender topic."

RICHARD C. SCHWARTZ, PH.D., FOUNDER OF
INTERNAL FAMILY SYSTEMS

"An inspiring journey of trauma and triumph. A uniting of science and shamanism in transforming trauma and restoring wholeness."

JOACHIM BAUER, M.D., PROFESSOR OF MEDICINE
AND NEUROSCIENCE, UNIVERSITY OF FREIBURG AND
INTERNATIONAL PSYCHOANALYTIC UNIVERSITY, BERLIN

AN
AUTOBIOGRAPHY
OF
TRAUMA

A HEALING
JOURNEY

A Sacred Planet Book

PETER A. LEVINE

Park Street Press
Rochester, Vermont

Park Street Press
One Park Street
Rochester, Vermont 05767
www.ParkStPress.com

Park Street Press is a division of Inner Traditions International

Sacred Planet Books are curated by Richard Grossinger, Inner Traditions editorial board member and cofounder and former publisher of North Atlantic Books. The Sacred Planet collection, published under the umbrella of the Inner Traditions family of imprints, includes works on the themes of consciousness, cosmology, alternative medicine, dreams, climate, permaculture, alchemy, shamanic studies, oracles, astrology, crystals, hyperobjects, locutions, and subtle bodies.

Cataloging-in-Publication Data for this title is available from the Library of Congress

ISBN 979-8-88850-076-7 (print)
ISBN 979-8-88850-077-4 (ebook)

Printed and bound in the United States by Lake Book Manufacturing, LLC

10   9   8   7   6   5   4   3   2   1

Text design by Priscilla Baker and layout by Virginia Scott Bowman
This book was typeset in Garamond Premier Pro with Span Compressed used as the display typeface

To send correspondence to the author of this book, mail a first-class letter to the author c/o Inner Traditions • Bear & Company, One Park Street, Rochester, VT 05767, and we will forward the communication, or contact the author directly at **somaticexperiencing.com**.

Scan the QR code and save 25% at InnerTraditions.com. Browse over 2,000 titles on spirituality, the occult, ancient mysteries, new science, holistic health, and natural medicine.

This book is lovingly dedicated to
two significant pillars of my journey.

First, to Laura Regalbuto, whose unwavering editorial
guidance has been a beacon throughout this endeavor. Her
astute challenges to areas of inconsistency
or ambiguity in my thoughts have been
truly indispensable.

Second, to my dear friend Butch Schuman,
who has tirelessly supported agencies that promote
the healing of traumatized children.
He left the world a better place.

Contents

Why Write This Book?

Although I have spent considerable time in the public eye, those closest to me can affirm that I am naturally shy and, sometimes, awkward. I am also a very private person, and thus I often feel hesitant to step into the spotlight or draw attention to myself. So in choosing to write this book and expose a great many intimate details of my life, I am left feeling unprotected and vulnerable. Even more distressing, as I shall shortly describe, is the fact that my being noticed could once have been life threatening, both for myself and my birth family. Hence from childhood onward, I have been afraid to stand out or be conspicuous.

The writing of these pages was originally meant to serve as a private excavation of hidden and disowned parts of my past and myself, and then to help me piece them together so I could fully own and embrace them. As I struggled mightily with the decision of whether to share my story with you, I had a dream: I am standing at the edge of an open field. In my hands, I hold a stack of typewritten pages. As I gaze out onto the meadow, I feel a strong breeze coming from behind me. I lift my arms and toss the pages to the wind, to land where they may. And so, my dear reader, I offer these personal and vulnerable pages from my heart to yours. I invite you to accompany me on this troubled and challenging yet ultimately empowering healing journey.

My desire is for this memoir to act as a catalyst for you, illustrating through my feelings and narrative, how one can achieve peace and wholeness even after devastating trauma. I hope that my story might encourage you to tell yours. It is my strong conviction that we all have valuable stories to tell and that telling them can help us grow and heal.

Finally, I ask myself: If a story told is also a life lived, then once I tell it, can I let it go? In deciding to toss these pages to the wind, I do so both for myself and for you as my witnesses and engaged readers. So let me begin with some of my beginnings.

Because this book is about raw trauma, it may bring up difficult sensations, emotions, and images in the reader. If so, I hope that you will take this as an opportunity for professional guidance. For Somatic Experiencing practitioners, please visit: www.traumahealing.org.

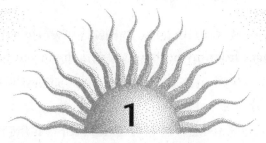

Born into a World of Violence

An Unfolding Story

We all have our stories to tell, and this is mine. It is my truth. Like Russian nesting dolls, it is one story contained within several others. As my good friend Ian said, "the shortest distance between two points is not necessarily a straight line." This memoir of nested stories is about my soul's journey. It is the often lonely path taken by an unsuspecting, unlikely, and deeply flawed missionary.

One of the core tenets of the trauma healing method I've developed over the past fifty years is that we don't ask people to confront their traumas directly. Rather, we gently encourage them to come to the periphery of these difficult sensations, emotions, and images and help them access certain pivotal positive bodily experiences first. What follows is such an example of visiting some specific positive memories in preparation for coming to terms with a terrifying episode of sexual assault. So let's begin with a description of two of my anchoring, joyful childhood experiences. They were both tremendously exciting, yet also embodied safety and the warmth of generous love.

A Birthday Surprise

Though I had a childhood replete with violence and life-threat, there were a few times that I felt cherished and protected. I recall these two experiences that left me with a full, open feeling in my heart and an exuberant bounce in my legs. I believe that these sensory and emotional imprints helped me to survive what surely could have destroyed me.

On the morning of my fourth birthday, I awoke to a grand treat. In the middle of the night my parents had quietly crept into my bedroom while I was sound asleep. Then, underneath my bed, and into the far reaches of the room, they stealthily laid the circular tracks for a Lionel model electric train set.

Can you imagine my delight when I awoke to the train clanging as it chugged around the tracks? Instantly, I jumped out of my bed and ran over to the transformer, where I could control the speed of the train. I beeped its horn with glee. I believe that this surprise gave me a sense of wonder and of being loved and cared for. Reflecting on this memory, I am reminded of an even earlier time when I felt tremendous and exuberant joy at being embraced and made to feel extra special.

When I was around the age of two, my father was the head counselor at a New England summer camp. Evoked by a black and white photo, I have a "body memory" of him standing in the swimming pool. I recall running and jumping into the pool. He made sure that I didn't drown as the water covered my sinking body. I can still sense his hands gently closing in around my hips, lifting me above the water, and depositing me on the grass at the edge of the pool. I would then ready myself by backing up and running, again and again, full speed across the lawn and jumping into the pool and my father's welcoming arms. After many of these flying jumps, the water quickly became my friend. My father would then gently hold my outstretched arms and let me lay on my belly and kick as I made my first swimming movements. After this introduction, I fell in love with swimming. Later, as an adult, I'd always find myself seeking places, on a lake or at the sea, any place where I could once again be held by the water.

Holding these "body memories" of being cared for helped make it possible for me to encounter many times of great distress, without being completely overwhelmed and annihilated. In later years, these memories supported my healing journey in resolving the following trauma.

In a Moment
of Violent Terror

When I was a child and adolescent, my family suffered prolonged life-threatening intimidation from the New York mafia. My father was called as a witness to testify against Johnny "Dio" Dioguardi, a ruthless mafioso of the Lucchese crime family.* In an attempt to protect my mother, me, and my younger brothers from almost certain death, my father refused to testify against Johnny Dio, even as this was demanded by the young and ambitious Robert F. Kennedy, then chief counsel to the New York Senate committee on racketeering. See plate 1 for a photo of Johnny Dio that is clearly worth a thousand words.

To help secure my father's silence, I was brutally raped at the tender age of about twelve years old by a gang belonging to the Bronx mob, likely the Fordham Daggers.† This violent incident happened under dense overgrown bushes in a neighborhood park, a place that had previously been a playground and treasured refuge for me. This rape was a secret that I kept hidden from everyone, especially from myself. It was buried in the recesses of my mind, but my body "remembered" it. Every day, as I walked to school, my body tensed and my breath constricted, as though my entire being was hyper vigilantly readying itself for another assault. But even more destructive than this was the ongoing fear, as I agonized about the disintegration of the very fabric of my family and, with it, the collapse of any enduring sense of safety.

I was never able to talk to my parents about this assault, as doing so would have confirmed the violence I endured. And so it became deeply lodged in my psyche as a pervasive sense of shame and

---

*Johnny "Dio" Dioguardi (who was mentioned in the mob films *Goodfellas* and *The Irishman*) was a vicious Italian-American organized crime figure and labor racketeer. He is known for being involved in the heinous acid attack that led to the blinding and disfiguring of newspaper columnist Victor Riesel. Riesel had been writing an expose on the New York mafia and the fake labor unions that helped Jimmy Hoffa become President of the Teamsters.

†In a Bronx website someone wrote that when I lived in the Bronx, prior to 1953, there was a gang called the Fordham Daggers. I was too young to know much about them except that everyone was afraid of them.

"badness." To displace these awful feelings, I assiduously avoided stepping on any cracks in the sidewalk, as I carefully walked the mile between school and home. I did this as if somehow I could ward off the threat with that classic ritual. In addition, I would constantly pray in the hope that God would protect me from another assault. I would place my hand over the top of my head, as covering the head was required by Orthodox Jews. I did this even though neither of my parents were practicing Jews in any regard. In fact, when my father saw me doing this, he would imitate and ridicule me. This humiliation was something I dreaded. As I reflect on this demoralization, I suspect it was his attempt to discourage me, and I believe that (at least in his mind) he was trying to "protect me" from doing this in public where I could be scorned. Unfortunately, it did not work. It only made matters worse. I felt both ridiculed and humiliated by him, while being left entirely alone with my crippling fear and anxiety.

It took forty years until I was able to access and release the "body-memory" of that brutal rape. I could then gradually restore a sense of enduring self-compassion and "goodness." What follows is how I unearthed and healed that memory.

A Wounded Healer

Fast forward many decades later. As I was evolving Somatic Experiencing (SE), my method for healing trauma, I mysteriously began experiencing persistent disturbing sensations and fleeting images. It felt like my throat and stomach were tightly constricted and clogged with a white viscous "gunk." As these alarming symptoms continued to plague me, I realized that it was high time I took a dose of my own medicine. As the saying goes, we always teach what we most need to learn. Chiron, the archetypal wounded healer, was calling for me.*

In reckoning with my distress, I humbly asked one of the teachers I had trained to help me untangle the possible origins of these troubling symptoms. The following remembrances began to emerge as I undertook an internal exploration. By focusing initially on my bodily sensations and then the disturbing images, some deeply buried inner movements began to emerge.

A Journey into Darkness

Trauma is not so much what happened to us, but, rather, what we hold inside, in the absence of an empathic, mutually connected, witness.

P.A.L., *In an Unspoken Voice*

What follows includes some vivid details of a violent rape, which may be disturbing to you. The reason that I have included these details (though probably difficult to read) is to illustrate that even after such an ordeal, given the right tools, and with competent

---

*In Greek mythology, Chiron was the son of the Titan Cronus and the water nymph Philyra, whom Cronus raped. Chiron was twice-wounded: once at birth, and again toward the end of his life. The first wound can be understood as a deep emotional injury from being a child of rape who was subsequently rejected by both of his parents. Apollo would assume the role of foster father. Being a centaur, Chiron was quite literally a monster, then an orphan, and ultimately an outcast. Being half-man, half-animal, Chiron embodies the conflict in all of us between our animal instincts and reason or divinity; between the Dionysian wildness of centaurs and the Apollonian order of his foster father. Yet he falls firmly on the Apollonian side, and in many respects outshines the god of light, mastering and even furthering the arts and sciences (*techne* and *episteme*) in an attempt to compensate for his early rejection and prove, both to himself and others, that he too is worthy of love and acceptance.

empathic support, it is possible to heal and put such traumas in the past, where they belong.

Sitting across from me, my colleague and guide took notice of a slight shuffling movement of my feet and gently brought my attention to this subtle, almost imperceptible, movement. Suddenly, an image of running freely on the oval track near my childhood apartment came to mind. My guide encouraged me to focus on the strength and power of my legs during that run. In Somatic Experiencing, we often evoke such inner strength to build sensations of empowerment, linked positive bodily experiences, before we gradually and gently excavate the trauma.

I felt my breath deepen and an expansive pleasure began to flow through my entire body. Gradually I looked around at this beloved landscape of my childhood refuge. I started to recall and describe my anticipation of its welcoming magic as I headed home from middle school each day. Usually, when I got home around 3:00 p.m., I would scarf down a handful of Pepperidge Farm chocolate mint cookies and take off on my routine excursion to the Reservoir Oval Park, which was located directly across from our six-floor Bronx apartment building at 3400 Wayne Avenue.

Rather than walking the two blocks to the park entrance, I would cross the road and scramble over the wrought iron fence, then head directly through the thicket of dense bushes to the running track below. There I would enjoy a surging power in my legs as I sprinted around the track. This triumphant release seemed to be an antidote for my unstable legs, which were weakened by the ongoing stress of my family's legal struggles and our fear of mafia violence. I could feel my legs alighting upon the cinder track, my slender, wobbly legs stretching out and gathering strength. Building on these powerful embodied "resource states," I would find a much needed strength and stability in the rhythm of that run. I exulted in this expansive memory. But then a more shadowy awareness began to seep into my recall. It was, initially, a nondescript uneasiness signaled by my uneven breathing and facial pallor. Thankfully, those earlier empowered resources gave me more confidence so that I could delve further into my encroaching distress.

Referencing one particular autumn day, I had a vague sense that something was amiss when I entered the park. I remembered catching sight of a few tough-looking teenage gang members, smoking cigarettes, and hanging out around those dense bushes. I particularly recalled their vintage motorcycle caps with leather peaks. In staying with these images, I noticed an ominous sense of lurking danger and felt a wrenching twist in my guts. Slowly, these procedural "body memories" started to emerge in much greater detail. First, I saw and felt myself taking a running leap over the fence and dropping down onto the other side, then navigating the steep slippery slope into the thick overgrowth of bushes.

Suddenly, despite my speed, I was overcome by a vivid and immediate sense of grave danger. Something was horribly wrong. What emerged in my awareness was a pervasive and overwhelming sense of threat. I experienced this as a gripping tension, a bracing, and stiffening in my neck and shoulders. I also felt this fear as a constriction of my breath along with a twisting and gripping in my guts. Abruptly and unexpectedly I jerked forward. I had yet another "body memory," one of being jumped from behind and thrown violently to the ground. I could feel my face smashed into the dirt with my forehead striking a large rock. I struggled mightily to get free. But it was all for naught, as my arms were pinned down and a heavy weight pressed painfully into my back. I was trapped like a helpless prey animal. Someone behind me started to tear at my clothing, pulling it and ripping off my pants. Immediately, I went blank. It seems that I passed out. Everything went very still, very quiet.

With extraordinary gentleness, my guide placed her hand on my shoulder and brought me back from the deep shock of that dissociation. I sensed the receding of that brutal violation and began to recover my sensory presence in the here-and-now. By the conclusion of the session, I discovered that my body could finally do what it couldn't do at the time of the rape. Indeed, one of the core principles of Somatic Experiencing lies in discovering new and more powerful experiences in our bodies, ones that contradict the feelings of overwhelming helplessness that are the hallmark of trauma. With the guidance of my therapist's expertise and presence, I began to sense my life force returning as I encountered a burning rage in my gut, then a surging power to fight back, and finally the fierce willpower to triumph over my attackers. I reconnected to the strength and vitality in my previously defeated arms and collapsed legs. Gradually, I began to sense the singular exhilaration I had known in leaping over the fence and running freely on the track. And then another "defensive response" reasserted itself with an involuntary revulsion emerging as a gag reflex. This was followed by a retching expulsion of what seemed to be a viscous fluid with a texture and smell similar to ejaculate.

This sequencing and the reworking of these very physical body memories resolved many of those symptoms that had prompted me to request the session. With self-compassion, I wept for the abused and discarded child, holding him in my arms with inner validation: "Yes, Peter, this really did happen. But it is over now."

In doing a few follow-up sessions, I was able to wrestle with the shame-demon and overcome my guilt and pervasive sense of badness. With tender feelings of genuine self-compassion and acceptance, I was able to place this memory in the distant past where it truly belonged. The "spell" was broken. I was free. I was alive. I felt whole.

More Remembrances

The truth changes color depending on the light, and
tomorrow can be clearer than yesterday.
Memory is a selection of images, some elusive . . . others
printed indelibly on the brain.

KASI LEMMONS, *EVE'S BAYOU*

In retrospect, and with the help of my brothers, I began to put the pieces of a narrative together. I found out from them that the mafia told my father: "You will find your family face down in the East River if you testify." Unable to obtain witness protection for the family, my father struggled against all odds, year after year, to avoid imprisonment for refusing to testify. In a case that eventually ended up in the U.S. Supreme Court, my father went to prison for "contempt of court." Chief Justice Earl Warren, in his dissenting opinion, wrote that this was one of the worst decisions the court had ever made. And so my father would serve a year-and-one-day sentence. This cruel and punitive extra day made it virtually impossible for him to ever return to teaching at a public school—an additional heartbreak for my father.

As you can imagine, this prolonged fear and uncertainty took a heavy toll on all of us. My sense of safety and faith in a sensible and predictable world was shattered. Yet, somehow, I was able to move forward, even though a disowned part of me was left in the violence of those bushes and the miscarriage of justice for my father.

It was an innocence lost, crushed, and desecrated but then, finally, recovered.

For a time after the session, I continued to visit "episodic" remembrances. However, they came without the emotional charge that had emerged in the potent session previously described. Here are some additional details I garnered. First, I was able to recollect how there had been an air of menacing darkness when a mafia lawyer would arrive at our house to meet with my parents. Ostensibly these visits were "to help" my father avoid testifying before the district attorney and the grand jury by pleading the Fifth Amendment. However, his real motives were to keep my father from fingering Johnny Dio.

I remembered crawling out of my bedroom and hiding beneath a narrow telephone table as I strained to hear their conversation in the living room. My parents never really talked to us kids about what was happening, but my younger brothers and I could sense, from their anxious body language, that something was seriously wrong. These undermining stressors and hidden conversations eroded my self-confidence and vitality. They were ultimately as injurious to my well-being as some of the more discreet, even devastating, traumas that I experienced throughout my childhood.

After fighting for many years, my father, unwilling to testify in order to protect his family, eventually surrendered to the authorities and began serving a year-and-a-day-long prison sentence. I was seventeen and a freshman at the University of Michigan when I received the news in a blunt unsentimental letter from my mother. I remember breaking down. Wrenching sobs ripped through my chest and dropped me to the floor with overwhelming spasms of guilt and grief.

Meanwhile, during my father's absence, his clothing business went bankrupt. With the weight of this profound stress, and the likelihood of encroaching poverty, my mother developed an ulcer and had some kind of "nervous breakdown." However, with the imperative of the family's very survival resting on her narrow shoulders, she pulled herself together and earned a teaching credential in order to support us while my father was in prison.

When I returned to New York City during spring recess, I visited my dad in prison. With the thick glass and metal bars between us, I was frozen with awkwardness. Not knowing what to say, I choked and swallowed the unsaid words, "I love you." Silently, as my mother and I walked out of the visiting area, a prison guard followed us and touched my shoulder. I turned around and met his unexpectedly kind eyes. He spoke softly, "I want you to know, son, that your father is not a criminal." He also told me that my dad had started a prison library and had taught other prisoners skills that they would need when they were released. In a twist of irony, my father had returned to his first love—teaching. My mother had followed in this tradition and later my brothers and I would continue this educational lineage, each in our own individual ways. I believe that this compelling desire to teach was passed to me and became my passion, perhaps, one might say, my obsession.

At one time, I met the principal of my mother's school. He took me aside and told me that my mother was the only teacher that could teach the most disturbed children. As an example, he described an autistic child that went into a closet even as the other children were going home. My mother patiently remained, waiting for over an hour, until the boy finally came out of the closet and let my mother hold and rock him. Though I didn't have any specific memories of her holding me in that way,

I could at least imagine what the principal described to me.

This profile of childhood distress and trauma was certainly not an unexpected antecedent to my brothers, Jon and Bob, and I combining this teaching instinct with a calling toward unconventional methods of healing. Though, as far as I know, there have not been any physicians in my ancestral line, I somehow intuit that we descend from a long line of rabbis, all (spiritual) healers in their own right. For me, this healing lineage was revealed as a life devoted to the study of stress and trauma and the innate drive for healing and wholeness. Indeed, it should probably be of no real surprise that my doctoral research, in medical biophysics, was on "Accumulated Stress."

In addition to the sources of corrosive stress I've already illustrated, punctuated by periods of abject terror, I also experienced more "ordinary" traumas throughout my infancy and youth. Of course, we will explore some of these along this journey of healing. A friend of mine once observed that "research is me-search." And so this has been my lifetime search, the alleviation of unnecessary suffering, the healing of trauma, not only for myself but for a world of countless injured people.

The Creative Force

The creative adult is the child that has survived.

PROFESSOR. JULIAN F. FLERON (THOUGH
OFTEN ATTRIBUTED TO URSULA LE GUIN)

In spite of these difficult beginnings I believe that, somehow, my parents always honored, respected, and promoted my innate impulse toward curiosity and exploration. In working with thousands of adults and many children, over a period of more than forty-five years, I have found that *all* children, and most adults with their younger selves still intact within, have this same innate pull of curiosity and exploration. It is this very vibrant impulse that can be harnessed to support our healing.

We all have the capability to heal. I believe there exists in humans a fundamental, primal drive toward wholeness and health. This includes access to a part of ourselves that has always been within, that lives beyond any trauma, and is eternally whole and undamaged. It is a part that could be called the True Self or Real Self. The Jungian analyst James Hollis defined the Self (with a capital S) as "the purposiveness of the organism, the teleological intention of becoming itself as fully as it can."[1] I would only add that this drive is to become more like our True Self, more like who we really are, outside of our roles and personas. In my experience, this drive is akin to that innate impulse toward curiosity and exploration.

Sadly this primal instinctual energy is all too often forced underground by oppressive oversocialization, or overwhelmed by toxic stress and trauma. Nevertheless, this powerful resource lives deep within all of us and lies in wait, ready to be awakened at the right moment. In spite of pervasive trauma, I believe this creative curiosity, and inner sense of vitality and exuberance, was always present in my life and is what helped take me from *there* to *here*.

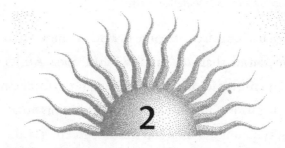

2

Healing with Science and Shamanism

Here and Now (A Sneak Preview)

People have sometimes described my healing work as being almost mystical or shamanic. While I certainly have been influenced by cross-cultural studies about shamanic healing practices and I have had opportunities to meet with various shamans and indigenous healers throughout the world, it has nevertheless been my lifetime task to prove that such labels are too elusive and woefully insufficient. In other words, my aim has been to demonstrate that the approach I have developed can be taught and practiced in Western secular society. The biological tradition that led me to this work has its origins in the highly "objective" sciences. Only later did my access to embodied spirituality organically emerge from a rock-solid foundation of biophysics, neurobiology, and ethology,* combined with complexity theory and systems theory.

Around 1972 I began teaching my healing approach to a dozen

---

*Ethology is the study of wild animals in their natural environments.

bright Berkeley therapists, during biweekly meetings held at my Wildcat Canyon "tree house" at 6182 McBryde Ave. Today, fifty years later, I may finally have completed my task of proving that this form of healing is not simply derivative of my individual gifts. Rather, the evolving healing method, currently called Somatic Experiencing (SE), named for the experience of the sensing, living body, is indeed scientifically based, teachable, and transmissible. One of the challenges in teaching SE, as well as researching its effectiveness, is that the method is not exclusively formulaic or a codified protocol, but rather an unfolding organic process that involves basic principles and building blocks. Despite this hurdle, however, a number of scientific studies have demonstrated that its mode of operation leads to strong, solid clinical efficacy.

In any case, from its inception with the "dirty dozen" in my humble tree house, the work has spread worldwide. By 2022 its reach had extended to forty-four countries through the diligent work of more than seventy international instructors. Together they have trained over 60,000 practitioners. As I reflect on this explosive growth and upon the trajectory of my life, I find myself truly dumbfounded. I have, without realizing it, become something akin to an unsuspecting and unlikely "prophet."

To the question of whether I have done enough, I can answer with a gentle "yes." Indeed, the responsibility of bringing this work to a troubled world now rests on the shared shoulders of the dedicated international SE faculty.

And what about the more elusive question, "Am I enough?" Of this conundrum, I must unburden myself, for I am simply a work in progress. Writing this book, for me, has been a way to collect my thoughts, memories, dreams, and reflections. The "am I enough" query relates deeply to my struggles with opening myself to love and accepting the feeling of being loved. I have often searched for the love of the "magical other" in an effort to find the one who would release me from my wounds. Along that road, I have been gifted with a number of precious woman lovers, as well as deep and persistent friendships from both genders.

But back to 1972. At our small Berkeley haven of kindred spirits, it was my job and our shared task to explain the how, what, and why of my support and facilitation for individuals who wished to heal their overwhelming stress and traumas. We were also trying to uncover a means by which our healing techniques could be methodically and holistically taught to others. At that time I was working on my interdisciplinary doctorate in the medical and biophysics departments at UC Berkeley. Hence, I was steeped in the fascinating world of the hard sciences including quantum physics, mathematics, and biology. I had a special interest in the nervous system and brain function. These explorations helped me understand the autonomic or involuntary nervous system, the upper brain stem, the cerebellum, and the limbic system. These are anatomical features we share with other mammals, and which give rise to, underlie, and shade all our sensations, emotions, and perceptions. These basic systems also shape many of our core beliefs.

Bottom-Up

As I evolved my body/mind approach, rather than utilizing a hierarchical, top-down system typical of traditional academic "talk" and cognitive behavioral therapies, I explored a "lower-archical" or bottom-up understanding. This process involved beginning the therapeutic work by engaging with bodily sensations as well as inner motor impulses and drives. In the words of the Kybalion, the Hermetic philosophy of ancient Egypt and Greece, "As below, so above." My approach aspired to unite the two routes, bottom-up and top-down, body and mind, into a holistic process that respected the totality and innate wisdom of the living human organism. In other words, I formulated a method that could guide those seeking healing to pay attention to their own somatic bodily experiences, along with the emotions and meanings we attach to our interoceptive bodily "landscapes."

We Are All Animals

For me, the icing on the cake, that delicacy of scientific inquiry, was my fascination and appreciation of ethology, the study of wild animals in their natural environments. Ethologists' respect for nature gave me an unexpected and juicy clue as to how individuals are traumatized and, more importantly, how we can heal. I began to use the ethological methodology of naturalistic observation with my clients. Like the ethologists, I would take note of people's subtle gestures, involuntary postures, facial expressions, heart rates, respiratory (breathing) rhythms, and skin color changes. All these are indicators of autonomic activity and precursors to feelings and eruptions of emotion. After all, we humans are mammals, albeit special ones, but mammals just the same! And as my childhood hero Yogi Berra, the famous 1950s catcher for the New York Yankees, put it: "You can observe a lot just by watching." And that is exactly what I did—month after month, year after year, decade after decade. I continued to emulate the great ethologists I had come to admire so deeply, particularly the research of Nikolaas Tinbergen, who shared the 1973 Nobel Prize in Medicine and Physiology.* From 1974 to

---

*See "Nikolaas Tinbergen Facts" on *The Nobel Prize* website.

1977 I corresponded with Tinbergen, then a professor at Oxford University, by "snail mail" and by phone via the new transcontinental underwater cables. This precious communication cost me much of my monthly graduate student stipend, as this was long before the expediency of cell phones and the internet. I was struggling with the doubt that I might just be imagining my observations and their significance for health, stress, and dis-ease. Tinbergen's acknowledgment and support buoyed me as I continued my pursuits.*

At the same time, I had a major setback in my academic progress. The chairman of my thesis committee, leading cell biologist Professor Richard Strohman, said I would only receive my doctorate over his dead body. He bluntly informed me that my work bridged too many disciplines to be valid and truly scientific. This was during the period, mind you, when I was in an interdisciplinary program at UC Berkeley called Medical and Biological Physics. It was a graduate school arrangement that allowed a few of us to study different, though potentially related fields. For me it involved a synthesis of biology, physiology, ethology, brain research, a branch of mathematics called catastrophe theory, and systems theory. Strohman's categorical rejection of my dissertation left me utterly despondent and not knowing where to turn.

I Give Thanks for Help Unknown, Already on Its Way

Thankfully, my dear friend Dr. Ed Jackson, who during that time was an adjunct faculty member at the School of Public Health at UC

---

*During this time, I also received some additional encouragement from Raymond Dart, the anthropologist who first discovered *Australopithecus* on the African savanna—the transitional "ape-man."

Berkeley, was also allowed to serve on the committee. Ed came to my defense and suggested we send my dissertation to leading researchers in each of the above fields. After a couple of months passed, with no response, I gave up in resignation and began to apply for a new doctoral program in psychology. But then on a sunny November day, a friend told me how she had been a guest at Professor Strohman's house for one of his infamous parties. Speaking from the sixties: the professor had a penchant for tall blonds, fine wines, and vintage Porsche convertibles. In any case, at the party my friend overheard a conversation between Professor Strohman and a young graduate student who was interested in studying stress. The student wondered if there were any seminars in that particular field. To that question, Strohman replied that she should speak with his "protégé" Peter Levine. Yes, those were his actual words! This juicy gossip meant I could celebrate that I was finally in the clear and could breathe again. I could at last move forward in my academic and scientific career.

When I next met with Strohman, he sheepishly congratulated me, as he had received several accolades from field leaders about "his" graduate student. One commenting scientist was Hans Selye, the innovative developer of the physiological concept of stress, who made significant contributions to science's understanding of the body's short- and long-term responses to stress and "strain." As a young medical student, Selye had also been marginalized by his clinical professors when he observed there were more similarities than differences across a diverse set of diseases with which his professors' patients had been diagnosed. In an emperor-has-no-clothes moment, Selye observed they all simply *looked* sick. Essentially he reasoned they all looked that way due to the "wear and tear" of stress. In other words, he proposed that the effect of stress was like a bank ledger: you can continue to withdraw money until you are in the red. His hypothesis was that, just like a savings account, there is only so much you can withdraw. When the reserves run out, your body becomes bankrupt. You then become sick, just like the many patients he had observed in medical school.

In my 1976 doctoral dissertation, however, I argued against this passive bank-ledger view of stress. I began instead to develop the concept of core resilience as a dynamic antidote for accumulating stress. In my thesis I argued strongly against Selye's concept of the human body as a financial account or bank ledger with only finite resources. I demonstrated, rather, that whenever we face threat or danger, our autonomic nervous system activates, or "charges." However given the right conditions, the nervous system rebounds and "dis-charges" this eroding activation. This dynamism restores equilibrium, internal regulation, and balance, and thus promotes overall resilience.

I also had a unique window into stress resilience when I lived a lifelong dream of working for NASA. Around 1978 I had the rare opportunity to work as a stress consultant to NASA, in a joint consortium with UC Berkeley on the early development of the space shuttle program. It was my assigned task to monitor the physiological squiggles, including heartbeat and respiration, that were sent back to Earth as the astronauts lifted off and then entered the microgravity of Earth orbit. At this point, a few of the astronauts would become nauseous and might even vomit. This "zero G sickness" was more than just annoying, it could damage the electronics and cause a potentially catastrophic malfunction. My assigned task was to monitor these physiological signals so as to predict when the vomiting might occur and then, of course, develop strategies to help stop it. Thus while I was seeing many of my clients become overwhelmed by stress, I saw the opposite response with most of the astronauts. The riveting question that emerged for me was: Is it possible to help "train" the autonomic response of my clients to develop core resilience, so they too can rebound like the astronauts did?

When Selye read my doctoral dissertation, he had the grace and humility to correspond with me. He did this even though I had argued against much of his basic theory, at least with regard to the capacity for resilience as an antidote to what he had called the "wear and tear" of stress. In a letter to Professor Strohman, he magnanimously wrote that my concept of resolved versus accumulated stress was a major contribution to a comprehensive understanding of stress. I would hope, likewise, to have some small degree of humility when someone, perhaps a student or colleague, challenges any of my theories or practices.

With gladness and appreciation, Selye and Tinbergen provided me with a foothold into a theoretical basis for my clinical observations. This gave me the confidence to immerse myself in this inquiry for many decades. With their generous support and encouragement, I would thus continue to explore my investigations, vision, and theoretical conclusions, despite my many apprehensions and insecurities. For that reason, I am sincerely thankful to both Professor Tinbergen and Dr. Selye, who together provided me with a contribution beyond measure.

Albert and Me:
Conversations at the Beggar's Banquet

I have never waited for invitations.

ALBERT EINSTEIN (TO MILEVA, FROM
THE OTHER EINSTEIN, A NOVEL BY MARIE BENEDICT)

Along my journey in learning how to help traumatized people recover their resilience, I also garnered some rather extraordinary help from an unexpected source: an apparition of Albert Einstein.

During the 1970s I envisioned that this unexpected and uninvited guest had paid me a visit. I had been working diligently on my theoretical biophysics doctoral dissertation on accumulated stress, as well as developing my body/mind approach to the resolution, prevention, and healing of chronic stress and trauma symptoms. After long, exhausting workdays, I would frequently visit my favorite restaurant, the Beggar's Banquet, located on San Pablo Avenue in Berkeley. Here, the warm and friendly waitresses always greeted me personally. My habitual dinner started with their homemade soup du jour, accompanied by a few slices of warm, crispy French bread.

Early one evening I was sitting alone at my usual table, a simple table for two. As I was savoring my vegetable soup, a shadow flashed by in my peripheral vision. Curious, I looked up from my dinner. Standing off to one side was an image of a disheveled, elderly man with curly and unkempt white hair. In my daydream he was wearing a crumpled, oversized sports jacket that dwarfed his slight frame. At first I was unnerved by this sudden apparition. But when I relaxed and opened to its presence, I recognized my idol, Albert Einstein! So I invited him to sit down across from me. Thus began a year of biweekly visits with this entity.

On the one hand, my rational mind recognized this image as an encounter with some unconscious, archetypal imaginative process, an example of what Carl G. Jung called "active imagination."* But

---

*Active imagination is a method for visualizing unconscious issues by letting them act themselves out. It can be used to bridge the gap between the conscious and unconscious minds. Active imagination is not meditation, self-hypnosis, guided imagery, or wish fulfillment, but is rather a way to activate the unconscious, and to have a dialogue with it, in an interactive, responsive way.

on the other hand, these manifestations seemed so thoroughly real, it was as though Albert Einstein himself were paying me these most welcome visits. In any case, these visitations supported my academic work and insights into the effects of stress. I highly valued these inner conversations that allowed me to access information from the "collective unconscious." See plate 2.

Such dinner encounters went on for about a year, as I chose to enter into that realm of active imagination. So genuine did these imagined encounters seem, I sometimes ordered two soups, one for myself and one for the professor, albeit not without a self-effacing chuckle at my own eidetic creative imagery.* At times the waitress would ask if I wanted her to bring out the second soup later so it would be warm. Somewhat sheepishly, I would decline and hope she didn't ask why. At our dinner meetings I would explore my deepest inner thoughts and nagging questions, particularly about my doctoral investigations into catastrophe theory, an esoteric branch of mathematics. This way I was able to model the nervous system's response to threat and stress. I imagined Einstein listening attentively, often with his head cocked sideways. He would then ask me questions about my questions. These Socratic-like exchanges would often open new vistas and deeper understandings. Ursula K. Le Guin, the lyrical and compelling writer, echoed this important truth about posing the "right" questions when she wrote, "There are no right answers to wrong questions."

Even today, more than forty years later, I reflect gratefully upon those vivid and revealing inner conversations with the mischievous professor. I am now bolstered by knowing I carry with me the ability to question my questions, while opening gradually to the answers. The writer Rainer Maria Rilke encouraged me to embrace my ques-

---

*Eidetic signifies a vivid, life-like image.

tions, when he wrote to a young aspiring poet: "Be patient toward all that is unsolved in your heart and try to love the questions themselves. . . . Do not now seek the answers, which cannot be given you because you would not be able to live them. And the point is, to live everything. Live the questions now. Perhaps you will then gradually, without noticing it, live along some distant day into the answer."[1] And I did just that for the next forty-plus years.

About thirty-five years ago, while visiting my parents in the Bronx, I happened to glance upon a bookshelf and noticed Einstein's *Relativity: The Special and General Theory.* This provoked me to tell them about my earlier "visitations" with the physicist. My mother sat up abruptly and uttered the words: "Peter, I know why this happened for you!" She went on, "When I was eight months pregnant with you, your father and I were canoeing when a wind squall swept across the lake and capsized our canoe." As she remembered it, the two of them had struggled unsuccessfully to right the canoe and were sure to perish. But just then, a young woman and an old man in a small sailboat came upon them struggling to upright the canoe. These newcomers, seeing my parents were in great danger, pulled them to safety. After offering towels for my parents to dry their shivering bodies, the rescuers introduced themselves as Albert Einstein and his stepdaughter! My mother reasoned—and she could be remarkably intuitive—that I had, somehow, bonded with Einstein during that intense moment of life-threat and subsequent salvation. I now recognized how and why the professor became my inner guide. All this time he had remained in the wings, ready to be called upon when I struggled with incomplete ideas or nagging doubts.

I stand by the veracity of this conversation with my mother without any doubt or equivocation. Both my parents confirmed their brush with death in the canoe, as well as the very real rescue by

Einstein and his stepdaughter. It is clear to me that this conversation with my mother exists in my memory as an ordinary recollection, not a figment of my imagination, in contrast to the vivid eidetic encounters with Einstein. Those stimulating "dinner conversations" seemed somehow to be downloaded to me from a universal, collective source. Perhaps I inherited some intuitive capacities from my mother that gave the apparitions this lifelike quality. In any case, Einstein remained a fruitful internal guide and mentor.

I must admit, however, that I became more intrigued by the mystery of this "channeling." I wondered how one might connect with such compelling inspiration without one's life being threatened. As I later came to comprehend, we are all informed by energy fields, which are themselves embedded within larger energy fields and connected to the energy fields of our ancestors and other important persons, as well as to the "macrocosm." Furthermore, these fields carry within them all the knowledge and great wisdom of the ages. This universal source of knowledge has been called the Akashic Records and was alluded to in the 1883 book *Esoteric Buddhism* by Alfred Percy Sinnett. Even today I am endlessly curious about the many access points to these universal records. I remain awed at how often the body's innate wisdom can serve as one of these conduits.

Without Einstein and his stepdaughter, I would not exist today in a physical body. My parents would have drowned, and I would have perished in utero. Yet I owe more than my life to Einstein. I have been profoundly blessed by his vast genius and willingness to take me under his virtual protective wing. With sincere appreciation in my heart, I feel tears of gladness moisten my eyes as I pen these words.

However emotional I may get in recalling this eidetic relationship, I also want to add that it is not unusual for an adult with an active imagination to be considered childish. While it might seem apparent that the need for creativity ends as one becomes a reasonable adult, I'd argue that creativity and imagination are just as important, if not necessary, to adults and children alike, especially with regard to our mental and emotional health.

Curiosity ____ the Cat

I have always had a fervent curiosity about science and nature, about how and why things work the way they do. I was the persistent and sometimes annoying child who always asked "why?" And while I faced a great deal of trauma throughout my childhood, both my parents enthusiastically supported my interest in nature, science, and what constitutes life. I feel immense gratitude toward Helen and Morris for their unwavering encouragement, and for the precious gift of life. They played a key role in cultivating my appreciation for both science and art. Moreover, their aiding of my relentless quest for "how and why?" guided me toward my eventual discoveries.

In 2010, I found myself being honored as the recipient of the first of four lifetime achievement awards. These awards have caused me to reflect from whence my knowledge and opportune gifts came from. How was it that I became the bearer of some long-forgotten but universal truths, an embodied knowledge of trauma and healing? Indeed, how had I fallen into the role of a truly unwitting crusader, an unsuspecting "prophet"?

Much to my surprise, my brother Jon appeared at the lecture hall for my acceptance speech. I have always felt that Jon didn't regard my work as being truly scientific and therefore viewed it as less valid. And so I was deeply moved when I spotted him in the audience. I will add here a few words about Jon, who holds an M.D., as well as a Ph.D. in neurobiology.

In 1978 as I was evolving my own work, Jon made a major medical and biological discovery. Briefly, it had long been known that a sugar pill administered to someone in acute physical pain could sometimes have a robust effect in blunting their pain if they were told the pill was a powerful pain medication. This pain relief from the ingestion of a sugar pill, called a placebo from the Latin root "to please," can be as powerful as the numbing effect of morphine, the gold standard of pain relief. Somehow this powerful self-healing effect had escaped scientific examination and explanation.

With his discovery of the placebo mechanism, Jon refuted the misbegotten notion that the placebo effect was simply a "psychological need" to please the all-important physician. Instead, it was a self-healing mechanism of paramount importance. Through this realization, he opened up the emerging field of self-healing, now called psychoneuroimmunology, which is essentially the science of the powerful body/mind interaction.

Jon knew from earlier research that there are special opioid receptors in the brain, as well as specific molecules called endorphins. These are released within the brain and then attach to those receptor sites. Jon reasoned that these are the same receptor sites where morphine, when administered externally, would also attach. Jon used naloxone* to block those specific receptor sites and showed that the placebo response was greatly diminished or completely blocked. Wow! What a fantastic and affirming discovery. Indeed this confirmed the actual *physio*logical rather than the assumed *psycho*logical explanation of the placebo effect. It was a matter of the body changing the mind, and the mind, in turn, changing the body.

---

*Naloxone is an "opioid antagonist," which means that it attaches to opioid receptors in the brain and blocks the effects of opioids. Naloxone is routinely used to reverse an opiate overdose.

The mid-seventeenth-century Dutch philosopher Baruch Spinoza espoused a concept along the same lines when he famously wrote, "Whatever increases, decreases, limits, or extends the body's power of action, increases, decreases, limits, or extends the mind's power of action. And whatever increases, decreases, limits, or extends the mind's power of action, also increases, decreases, limits, or extends the body's power of action."

The broad discipline that Jon's work stimulated is concerned with receptors and molecules in the brain that can be mimicked by certain substances that are exogenous, or of external origin. These substances range from opioids to tranquilizers and antidepressants, and potentially also include psychedelics like LSD, psilocybin, ayahuasca (DMT), and ecstasy (MDMA). Perhaps these "mind-expanding" substances stimulate parts of the brain in a manner similar to endorphins, and are part of a larger system linked to a powerful drive toward wholeness and an evolution in consciousness and deep healing.

The question for me was how to access and harness this internal healing system, not only through the use of external drugs, but rather by enlisting the vast innate power and wisdom of the body/mind. In other words, there could be a variety of ways to access and therapeutically engage these powerful, endogenous neurotransmitters to evoke radical self-healing. During this search, I was surprised to also discover a strongly welded unity between the transformation and healing of trauma and various extraordinary or "peak" experiences and practices found in spiritual, meditative, shamanic, and mystical traditions throughout the world. To bear witness to such vast and enduring transformations of trauma has been a privilege beyond measure. It has been the driving force in both my professional and personal growth.

In studying the innate organismic mechanisms by which people heal, my brother Jon and I were truly more than blood brothers— we were scientific and clinical brethren pursuing the study of innate mechanisms that support spontaneous, organic intelligence and healing. I should also mention that my youngest brother, Bob, is a leading "healer of last resort" who utilizes Chinese and Tibetan medicine, acupuncture, and homeopathy for suffering patients when all else has failed. Mama would have been proud of all three of us!

Peter and the Cabbage Head

Understanding physics is child's play,
when compared to understanding child's play.

ALBERT EINSTEIN

At my acceptance speech for that first lifetime achievement award, I briefly mentioned my perpetual curiosity. Later, after the award was presented, I had lunch with Jon and he shared a salient memory he had retained from our childhood.

When I was six or seven years old, my grandfather bought a farm in upstate New York. This was a place where I felt a drive toward exploration and a sense of freedom and belonging. The farm was a respite from the extreme dangers of the city. I remember eating the fresh vegetables and fruit that were picked each day, and especially the apple pies my grandmother baked. My slice of pie would be topped with a strip of cheddar cheese from the local dairy farmer, and atop that, a dollop of vanilla ice cream.

What I most remember was going to the chicken coop in the morning and collecting eggs for breakfast. After doing so, I would set out on my daily adventures, carrying the sandwiches my grandma had made the night before. During this rite of passage I climbed over hills and tramped through forests, and only returned at dusk for a home-cooked meal. In this place of refuge I came to know the cycles of nature.

After some years, probably when I was about ten, while Jon was seven, and Bob was four and a half, our little trio, being the cute entrepreneurs we were, would load up our red wagon with a cornucopia of fruits and vegetables from the farm. Then, heading down the dusty dirt lane known as Pine Tree Road, we would sell them to the summer residents of a bungalow vacation colony a mile from the farm.

Imagine, if you would, three endearing boys making their daily rounds selling fresh-picked produce to the nearby summer encampment. One such warm and sultry day, we tramped back to the farm with an empty wagon save for one lone item, a head of cabbage. It was getting close to dinnertime, so after a short rest, we resumed our journey. I noticed that the head of cabbage, which was sitting in the front of the wagon, would seem to roll backward as we walked on.

According to Jon's rendition, I compelled him to repeatedly start and stop the movement of the wagon so I could sit by the side of the wagon and observe the fascinating behavior of the cabbage. In a spellbinding flash, I recognized that the cabbage did not move to the back of the wagon, but instead remained mostly stationary as the wagon lurched forward. That evening I told my mother about my observations, and I asked her why this happened every time. With a brief flicker of amusement, she said, "Peter, you've just discovered Newton's First Law of Motion."

So perhaps curiosity, rather than killing the cat, might have, as a mentor and friend named Dick Olney once said, "led the cat to realizing its highest and greatest potential." Many years later, in high school physics with Mr. Sheeran (who taught all three of us!), I was reminded again of Newton's First Law: that a body at rest tends to remain at rest unless acted upon by an outside force, and a body in motion tends to stay in motion unless acted on by an outside force. And oddly enough, this is personally relevant, as I have always been an object in motion: a peripatetic, endlessly curious rolling stone, undeterred by outside forces. Like Johnny Appleseed, for decades I traveled the world over, a vagabond and a relentless missionary, planting my seeds of knowledge among those who might be receptive, even when it seemed futile.

On a Bicycle (Re-) Built for Two and Five

When I was around the age of five, my father left his job as a high school teacher and principal, a role that had nourished both his heart and mind. He relinquished this passion and, to support his growing family, became a dress manufacturer in the rough, tough, mafia-infested New York garment district. This was a decision he later regretted, as it put our entire family in serious and prolonged jeopardy. But at the time all any of us kids knew was that rather than coming home in the late afternoon, he now came home between nine o'clock and eleven o'clock in the evening. When I was about six, I tried to stay up as late as I could, and when the doorbell rang I would rush to the door and jump into his welcoming arms. That moment of joy filled me with the heartening feeling of protection and goodness. I recall the exact sensation of his rough whiskers brushing against my tender face. However, despite his late work hours, he reserved one day of the week exclusively for our family to be together. Sunday was that special day.

When my father was in his early twenties (in 1936), he and a friend took the *Île de France*, a great ocean liner, from New York to Paris. There, they purchased a tandem bicycle and cycled together throughout France, and then on to Budapest, Hungary. After this odyssey, my father returned and brought the bicycle back home to the Bronx for our family to enjoy. Our Sunday mornings usually began with bagels, cream cheese, lox, pickles, and smoked white fish from the local Jewish delicatessen. Then, with full tummies, we would run down to the basement where that hallowed, maroon tandem bike was stored. My father had made some modifications to the old, well-seasoned bike. He had added extra seats: one just behind the front seat with an improvised handlebar, another jury-rigged on the rear baggage rack. Imagine this: Dad and Mom peddling the three of us brothers—me behind the front seat, Jon on the rear baggage rack seat, and baby Bob tucked snugly into the bike's front basket. People would file out of the neighborhood tenements and gawk at the sight of the five of us riding to Reservoir Oval Park. A lovely image. But mind you, like Reservoir Oval Park and so much of my early life, there was a dark and traumatic side to the bicycle's origin story.

Shadows of the Holocaust

Upon arriving in Budapest, my father Morris found his way to the home of some of his relatives. There he witnessed an elderly Jewish shopkeeper dragged from his bakery at the end of the street and mercilessly beaten by a group of Crossed Arrow hooligans. Hungary's right-wing Arrow Cross Party was nationalist to the extreme and modeled itself on Germany's Nazi Party but, compared to the S.S. Storm Troopers, these thugs were even more venomous and vicious in their antisemitism. My father readied himself to rush to the poor man's aid. But thankfully, his relatives grabbed his arm and restrained him from dashing forth. In broken English, they commanded, "Stop! Don't! You have to be crazy. They kill you both!"

Thus, in addition to the family bicycle, my father returned from his journey bringing home with him a horrific glimpse of the prelude to the Second World War. The specter of war had been looming on the horizon. Its menacing shadow was accompanied by the Nazi Holocaust, the slaughter of six million Jews alongside Catholics, Romani, homosexuals, the disabled, intellectuals, and other so-called "undesirables." The scourge of war and genocide was to shake the world to its very foundations—and my family's world as well. As a child I didn't understand why, aside from my father's parents Dora "Baba Dosi" and Grandpa Max, I had no other living relatives on his side of the family. This seemed particularly unsettling because, on my mother's side, I had not only my maternal grandparents but also aunts, uncles, cousins, and other relations. Apart from one cousin, all my father's family in Europe had been murdered by the Nazis.

After the war, around 1952, the Red Cross had a program to unite refugees with possible family members living in the United States. Somehow they found a young man who had escaped from Auschwitz and had been surviving for two years in the forests, living like an animal on berries, roots, and leaves—one of the Forgotten Jews of the Forest or, as I put it, Forest Jews.[2] Along with my parents and grandparents, we went to meet Zelig, a distant cousin and my only paternal family member in Europe to survive the Holocaust. I remember being utterly haunted by the blue numbers tattooed on his forearm, and by his mysterious, barely comprehensible foreign accent.

Unbeknownst to me back then, a short time after Zelig's unexpected visit, my paternal grandmother Doris "Baba Dosi" lifted her eighty-pound, frail, and cancer-ridden body to the window ledge of her apartment and jumped to a violent death six stories below. As I was eventually to realize, her suicide was a response to delayed survivor's guilt, possibly brought on by the visit of Zelig, her one and only remaining distant relation in the whole world. As I would also come to learn, these types of nightmarish traumas can be transmitted over multiple generations. Indeed these implicit memory engrams had a deep impact on my life, particularly on some of my behaviors, and my haunting and pervasive feelings of shame and guilt.

Around the time of my visits with Einstein, as I continued working with my clients' implicit—or bodily and emotional—sensory memories, I was taken by surprise when a few of them reported the acrid smell of burning flesh. This was particularly unexpected since many of these people had been longtime vegetarians. When I asked them to interview their parents regarding their family histories, a number reported that their parents or grandparents had been Holocaust victims or survivors. Was it possible these clients were somehow being impacted by a potent, racially specific, cross-generational transmission of their parents' and grandparents' trauma in the death camps? Given what was known about an individual's memory at that time, this explanation seemed highly unlikely.

I remained puzzled by the specificity of how the smells from the death camps could possibly be passed on through generations to my clients. But then I recently came across some startling animal experiments carried out by Brian Dias at Emory University School of Medicine in Atlanta. The researchers exposed a group of mice to the scent of cherry blossoms. I don't know if it was pleasant to them in the way it is to humans, but certainly it wasn't aversive. But then the experimenters paired the scent with an electric shock. After a week or two of such pairings, the mice would shake, tremble, and defecate in acute fear when exposed only to the cherry blossom scent. That result is really no surprise, as it is a common Pavlovian conditioned reflex. However—and I am curious about what motivated these scientists—they bred these mice for five generations. The denouement of these experiments is that when they exposed the great-great-great-grandchildren of the original mice pair to the cherry blossom scent, they shook, trembled, and defecated in fear just from the scent alone. These reactions were as strong as or even stronger than those of their great-great-great-grandparents who were initially exposed to the cherry blossoms paired with the unconditioned stimulus in the form of shocks. The mice did not react with fear to a wide variety of other scents—only to the cherry blossom smell! A final, interesting outcome of this study was that the fear conditioning was transmitted more robustly when the male, or father, was the member of the original mating couple exposed to the conditioned fear reaction. This specificity is something that didn't completely surprise me, as I had always felt that the Holocaust memories I myself encountered came primarily through my father—more on that later.

The clinical question regarding this transmission was how to help my clients heal from deep-rooted ancestral traumatization that was passed on from generation to generation. How could I enable these individuals, and myself, to heal from such alarming memory imprints when the trauma had never personally happened to us? This inquiry was also highly relevant for people of color and First Nations people.

When I first spoke publicly about these generational transmissions in *Waking the Tiger: Healing Trauma*, published in 1996, I was often criticized for making such preposterous suggestions. Today in 2023, however, an increasing number of research studies have confirmed such ancestral transmission and have even decoded the molecular basis for certain types of "epigenetic transmission," using animal experiments.

Recently, I came across the writings of an "old friend" who, long before such research existed, and well before my speculations on generational transmission, postulated a similar perspective on ancestral influences. Carl G. Jung, in his book *Psychological Types*, wrote: "all experiences are represented which have happened on this planet since primeval times. The more frequent and the more intense they were, the more clearly focused they become in the archetype."[3] This might be one reason why wars are never truly over, and why there are no "wars to end all wars."

At one of my final imagined dinner meetings with Einstein, I brought up these questions of ancestral trauma, particularly regarding my clinical observations of the children and grandchildren of the Holocaust, as well as some of my impressions with Black clients who seemed to be carrying the pervasive legacy of slavery, racial injustice, and exploitation on their shoulders and in their hearts. Then, in having the privilege of working with a few First Nations people, I perceived they also shouldered a great weight from their cultural genocide in the Americas.*

When I conveyed these musings to Einstein, I visualized him gasping as his face turned pale. He was visibly shaken by my discussion of the Holocaust, and it seemed to me that tears rolled down his cheeks. We both sat dazed and speechless. As in a dream, I imagined him leading me to a pond in a forest clearing, whose water was smooth as a mirror's surface. He placed a row of small stones on a yardstick, which he then held above the water. As we sat there

---

*These corrosive effects have been reinforced by both explicit and implicit current legacies of systemic racism, which still exist today and add to the burden of people of color in many parts of the world.

together, he tipped the yardstick and all the stones fell simultaneously into the water. This caused intersecting concentric ripples to move outward, expanding in space and time. If where the ripples intersected they somehow got "stuck," this would distort the movement of the entire wave pattern. In my reverie, Einstein called these fixations "ego points."* This was a strange term, but I did grasp his meaning. He went on to illustrate how, with each of these fixations, the wave fronts were then distorted from that point on, forever, if not completely altered. But how? How could enough of the fixated points be "neutralized" so the person could move from fixity to flow, from distortions to unimpeded expression and expansion? This transformation, as I was to learn, involved working with the "embodied energy patterns" that underlie ancestral transmissions. This discovery was also an important step in my own healing.

Returning from my reverie, I looked up from the table and imagined that our gazes met in a prolonged stillness. "Professor," I muttered to myself, breaking the silence, "in that case, the trick would be to somehow 'unstick' enough of these fixation points so the wave front would again become coherent, as the circles continued to move outward, expanding in space and time. Yes! But how to do this?"

"Peter," I envisioned him saying with particular emphasis, "I must leave that to you."

"Yes, Dr. Einstein. I think I can learn how to do this."

He replied, "Then you will not need me anymore; it is now in your hands." While I don't recall if this was our last meeting, it was

---

*One reason why Einstein might have used the term "ego points" was to refer to, and possibly confess to, his narcissistic and exploitive relationship with his first wife Mileva Marić. But that is indeed another story, and one I only learned about in the past ten years. At any rate, his personal shortcomings do not change the gift of my ("imagined") encounter with this great man of science.

near the end of our dinners together at the Beggar's Banquet. A celebration of bittersweet tears.

Conception Trauma

On one of my occasional trips to New York City, I mustered the courage to ask my mother if she had noticed any changes in my behavior around the time of the rape. When I briefly described what had happened that day in the park, my mother stiffened in defensiveness. I was taken aback when she blurted out: "Peter, I don't believe that rape really happened. Instead, your father raped me— that's how you were conceived." My jaw dropped in disbelief. What was she talking about? Was she denying my experience? She went on to explain that my father, to reduce his chances of being drafted to fight in World War II, had raped her to make her pregnant with me! I don't know why she brushed aside my rape to propose her own rape as the instrumental devastation. But, astoundingly, she believed she had passed her experience of being raped onto me at the very moment of my conception. At the instant when my father's sperm penetrated her ovum, this implantation was the beginning of my wounded life. A life in which I was fundamentally "bad," as I had ruined any opportunity my mother might have had to develop herself as a scientist, musician, and artist—a burden I carried for many decades.*

In working with thousands of individuals, it has been my consistent observation that not only are perinatal "imprints" possible, but that transgenerational, or ancestral, transmission of trauma seems

---

*When I first started psychotherapy, I had an important dream that spoke to the complicated relationship I shared with my mother. I will explore the dream more fully in chapter 4.

to occur both at the moment of conception and in the early perinatal period. But what was even more astonishing to me was how my mother sensed that her trauma from her perceived rape by my father was transmitted to me at the moment of my conception. Having listened to my mother's perspective, I nevertheless understood clearly that both our ordeals were genuine—I had indeed been raped in the park.

From my ongoing sessions with my colleague, I had vivid implicit or "body" memories of the event. In addition, around the time of my rape, I was plagued by extreme anxiety and obsessive-compulsive disorder (OCD)–like behaviors, assiduously avoiding stepping on sidewalk cracks and compulsively praying and pulling out my hair until I had small bald spots. I don't think my parents were observant of these behaviors; they assumed nothing was amiss, in spite of the pervasive threat to our family, hence my mother's dismissal of my story of the assault.

Her accusation against my father is corroborated by a report from one of my brothers, who has shared with me that my father also violated his sexual boundaries. When my brother finally confronted him, at his death bed, my father claimed he had done this to "bond" with my brother. As for my mother's belief that he had raped her, my father insisted, "I was just being very passionate, and maybe I lost control." This was his version of the story. But whatever the ultimate truth, it amazes me what complex webs we uncover in searching through the pieces of our lives, and how it takes patience and fortitude to gradually untangle this twisted ball of emotional yarn.

In reflecting on my mother's sobering intuition about my "conception trauma," I found her revelation distressing yet also illuminating and freeing. It helped me to better comprehend my struggle to feel at ease in this incarnation, to comfortably embody my existence in this lifetime.

My own injuries have also helped me to better understand the struggles of the many people who feel they don't belong in the world, or don't have a right to exist. These vague feelings appear to be unrelated to any specific traumatic events. The origins of such perinatal and conception experiences are elusive. But their compelling influence on our behaviors and emotions cannot be denied.

A few more thoughts regarding my mother: I wish to acknowledge that I have been gifted with some of her innate, intuitive wisdom. While I am grateful for this gift, it doesn't exonerate her from the coldness, dismissiveness, and neglect she displayed during my upbringing. My memories of being diminished and unseen have at various times brought on waves of fiery anger that emanate from my diaphragm. Yet this anger, when fully experienced as intense sensation, has brought me enlivenment, vigor, and power. It is what I call "healthy aggression," an important vehicle to forward movement in one's life—movement beyond the blockages and the wounds.

Had my mother been born around our current moment in history, she would likely be considered an "intuitive," one possessed of exceptional psychic abilities. So, Mother, I thank you again for sharing those precious gifts, these contributions that have supported my development and skills as a therapist and teacher.

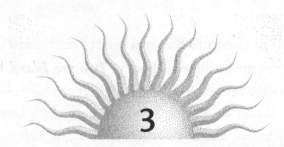

3

Dreams Show the Way

A Treasure to Be-hold

A dream, circa 1980: I am in a small room where I meet a man with a luminous presence. He wears a black robe, with purple sashes over his shoulders that flow down the front of the robe. He seems self-contained and deeply contemplative. The man approaches me slowly but deliberately. He is carefully holding an aged wooden box with a domed lid and two brass straps binding its girth. It is sealed shut with an ornate brass latch.

We face each other in silence. He then gently holds out the box, offering it to me. I take it and cradle it in my arms. He conveys, without words, that I have been tasked to carry it through a door leading into another room. At the far end of that room is a cast-iron safe with a combination lock. I understand that it is my responsibility to open the safe and place the box there—for "safekeeping."

Upon waking from this dream, I found myself deeply puzzled. So, as is my custom, I focused on the different images in the dream and then noted my body sensations and feelings. I shifted back and forth between those images and sensations and observed what was arising spontaneously. As I concentrated on the image of the box, I

42

was delighted to recognize that it was like the treasure chest from one of my favorite childhood books, *Treasure Island* by Robert Louis Stevenson. But what, I wondered, was the dream trying to tell me? What was I missing? Was there a code I somehow needed to decipher, as represented by the combination on the safe? Even more perplexing was the mystery of what was in the treasure box, and why it was my task to place it in the safe. But no matter how much I thought over these questions, I could not come up with any answers.

Later that week, while attending a party in Boulder, Colorado, I met a young woman named Elaine. After some polite chitchat, we established a feeling of personal connection. Our exchange evolved into a serious discussion of books, music, spirituality, life, and the work I had been developing.

I felt comfortable enough to recount my recent dream to Elaine. She seemed particularly interested in having me describe in detail the man who had presented me with the chest. Then, she motioned for me to follow her into a quiet room at the back of the house. In beautiful calligraphy, she wrote on an index card the name and phone number of a Tibetan Lama living in Berkeley, California. He had been a spiritual teacher of hers. I folded the card and placed it in my wallet. And there it remained.

A year or so later, I was in Berkeley teaching while staying with my friend and colleague Anngwyn at her house in Strawberry Canyon. I was searching for something in my wallet when the card with the Lama's name fell to the ground—seemingly a lucky "accident." I picked it up, chuckled, and decided to chance a call to the number on the card. One of the Lama's students answered, and I asked to speak with the Lama. Timidly I inquired if he would be willing to meet with me. He kindly agreed, so I promptly called a cab. Twenty minutes later I arrived, and he welcomed me by offering a cup of tea.

I told him that Elaine, his former student, thought the work I had been developing might share common ground with Tibetan Buddhist traditions. As I described my theory and practice, the Lama listened attentively, poured another cup of tea for the two of us, and nodded gently. Finally, he said, "What you've described has much correspondence with the Kum Nye* tradition in Tibetan Buddhism." However, he went on to explain, that the principles I had outlined were "more universal than one single tradition," and had evolved from many healing methods used throughout the world over the ages. He added one last thought: that this enduring wisdom probably originally derived from Celtic Stone Age religions.

Later that day, I made haste to the Berkeley University library and began researching information on Celtic Stone Age religions. There I discovered an image of Newgrange, a temple built in 3200 BCE, well over five thousand years ago. To enter the inner sanctum, a visiting pilgrim must pass a guarding stone inscribed with paired vortices. From the image, it seemed there was also a third vortex, perhaps indicating the holding awareness of both vortices. See plate 3.

The image instantly revealed to me the meaning of my dream. I now understood, with total clarity, that my task in this lifetime was to help keep this ancient wisdom alive—to keep it in a safe place. The significance of the dream image, in which I placed the treasure box in the safe at the back of the room, was now apparently clear. My life's work was in uncovering the code: finding a current biological and neurophysiological understanding of healing and transformation. This repackaging of ancient, preliterate, shamanic

---

*The main tenet of Kum Nye is that, for the skilled practitioner, all the universe is to be found within the felt interiority of the body, in the form of more and more subtle physical sensations. In Somatic Experiencing, similar levels of sensation are evoked in the "renegotiation" of trauma.

knowledge, and the recapturing of its universal wisdom, would allow this knowledge to remain relevant in today's world dominated by scientific thinking. I was, it seemed, entrusted with the task of keeping this perennial treasure safe for current and later generations.

As I meditate on this lifelong endeavor, I can see it has been a privilege and a gift, an outsized mission, and a treasure beyond compare. Yet at times it has also been a lonely trek, a backbreaking burden to lift, and a confining duty. It has often taken precedence over personal relationships, and even over marriage and a family. Though thankfully I have been blessed with my wonderful godchildren Alana Rose, Ossian, Jacob, and Jada.

An Earlier Dream (circa 1964)

The right way to wholeness
is made up of fateful detours
and wrong turnings.

CARL G. JUNG

I recall another dream, more than fifteen years earlier: A man is driving a 1948 Hudson convertible car on the Hudson River as though it were a boat. As he goes underneath the George Washington Bridge, he looks up at the sky, shakes his fist, and loudly commands, "God, if you exist, then give me a sign!" But he doesn't realize the left turn signal, located at the base of the steering column, is blinking with a small green light.

For those who don't know, the Hudson is an automobile that was manufactured in the 1940s. The cars at that time did not have signal turn lights. So to signal other drivers of their intentions, the driver had to use hand signals to indicate whether they planned to make a right or left turn or were coming to a stop. Around this time, it became possible to jury-rig an apparatus by mounting a turn switch near the lower part of the steering column. This switch would then be wired to lights mounted on the back of the car. The blinking light (signaling a turn) was mounted on the steering column, and would only be visible if you were paying attention to it. I believe this type of awareness is how we tune into synchronicities.

From this dream, I came to understand that at different times in my life, God has spoken to me, but I often didn't listen to Her guidance. Taking these messages more seriously and conscientiously has led me through what Carl G. Jung called "synchronicities." These meaningful coincidences—or co-incidents—have guided me personally, professionally, and spiritually. I suspect my conversations with Albert Einstein were an example of my being touched by these numinous creative forces, and being led in directions my conscious mind could not fully grasp at the time.

The question of whether these encounters with Einstein were real or not misses the essential point. These visitations and conversations were absolutely real in terms of what Jung called the collective unconscious. Perhaps they also were aligned with what have been labeled the Akashic Records, as mentioned in chapter 2. These are a chronicle, a compendium, of all human events, thoughts, words, emotions, and intentions ever to have occurred in the past, present, or future. They are believed by theosophists to be encoded in a nonphysical plane of existence known as the "mental plane." I would suggest that these records are also embodied in the space-time energy/knowledge/wisdom fields where Albert and I met for our conversations at the Beggar's Banquet. The most crucial inquiry is determining how to access this domain of inner wisdom through dreams and coinciding synchronicities. As in my dream, it is essential to be aware when the signal light is blinking for one's attention!

To return to my dream of being tasked with guarding the treasure chest: I realized this was another instance of my listening to God and receiving Her divine guidance in the form of images, dreams, and gut feelings. These intuitive awakenings are what have allowed me to midwife, birth, and caretake my life's work, a gift to myself and to humanity.

In order to keep SE safe, as in my dream, I have been impelled to focus on the scientific and clinical components of SE and have not openly addressed its intrinsic spiritual dimensions. Yet in addition to an appreciation of the role of body sensations in healing trauma, I also have come to realize that out of body sensations arises a universe of mysterious and transcendent states, perhaps what Carl G. Jung called the *mysterium tremendum*—that great mystery of life itself. It seems this is what was understood and practiced within the form of Tibetan Buddhism called the Kum Nye tradition. In a later chapter, I will attempt to correct my long failure to address these important and compelling numinous experiences in my scientific work.

It has become abundantly obvious to me that many of the apparent "coincidences" I have encountered over my lifetime were in fact synchronicities. They were guidance from Spirit in my journey, although I was often oblivious to Its presence. As recently as the night before I write these words, I had one of these epic dreams which, upon waking, I failed to jot down in my dream book. Damn it! Nevertheless, I don't beat myself up for such lapses. If I can, through self-acceptance, immerse myself in Spirit's all-encompassing presence, I can look forward to the night's encounter with the dream-plane.

This brings to mind a lovely pilgrimage I once made with friends to the Abbey of the Black Madonna in Einsiedeln, Switzerland. At this time I was in direct contact with that deep feminine comforting presence: a reminder that she is and will always be there. As the Beatles song written by Paul McCartney intones: *When I find myself in times of trouble, Mother Mary comes to me / Speaking words of wisdom, let it be.* I know now that when I feel most alone, lost, and adrift, the goddess will be there to hold and comfort me, if only I can learn to trust in her embrace.

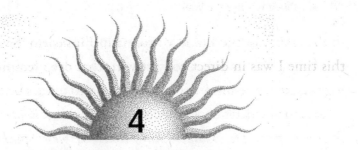

4

Hidden Tears:
A Psychedelic Opening

Grief is love with nowhere to go.

WAYNE GRIGSBY AND
LOUISE PENNY, *THREE PINES*

I offer another dream of mine as an exploration through which I aim to reveal a hidden, tender part of myself to myself. I hope my reflections on this dream will also be an invitation for you to accompany me on this part of my healing journey.

When I started my first psychotherapy sessions in 1964, I had this revealing dream: I was carrying a heavy log up a steep hill. I gripped the log at the front end; and at the rear, holding the other end, was my mother. We each had walkie-talkies in our hands. Above us was a frigid, snowcapped mountain peak. And at the top of the peak was the white-hot flame of an oxidized manganese blaze. The coldest place below; the hottest place above.

Later, as I pondered this upsetting dream, I was disturbed to realize the hefty log was a deep burden I'd carried my whole life, and that my mother had not really helped me with this burden, but instead had given me commands through her walkie-talkie. The ice-cold mountain and the searing flame were representative of my mother's intense extremes, her deep coldness and her volcanic heat. She could both freeze and scorch. Such was the crucible of our troubled relationship.

As much as I have suffered pain from her unpredictable extremes, I am equally saddened by the suffering I have caused some of my intimate partners, during times when I would turn on and then abruptly turn off. I am painfully aware of my tendency to alternately be remote and cold and then erupt with fire and passion. I yearn to transform this circle of pain into a circle of grace, forgiveness, and connection. Thankfully in my later years I have become more balanced in my affections and moods. Here, I will discuss some of my steps on that journey.

When my father's younger sister died, I distinctly remember seeing him well up with tears—the first and only time I ever saw him exhibit sadness, or any other emotion, except rare outbursts of anger or moments of happiness. For his sudden expression of grief and sorrow, my mother sternly rebuked him: "Morris, tears won't bring her back." Perhaps she was trying to help, but more likely her harsh words were due to her own lifelong suppression of her feelings. Either way, that moment in which she stifled my father's vulnerability had a lasting impact on me. When my parents told me that my dear aunt "Sunshe," a nickname for Sonia, had died, I ran to the bathroom and locked the door so my mother couldn't get to me. There I struggled alone with my grief. To avoid being frozen by my mother's harsh Medusa-like gaze, I learned to stuff down my tears whenever they arose.

A few years later, my dear Grandpa Max, an important attachment figure for me, died of a sudden heart attack. I can fondly recall how I would sit on his lap and play with his pocket watch, a gift he received in recognition for his work as a plumber building submarines for the Second World War, at the naval shipyard in Groton, Connecticut. I was assigned to be a pallbearer at his funeral. As we somberly walked out to the hearse, in haunting unison, I stifled my sobs of grief by biting down so hard on my lips that they bled.

Tears Reclaimed

As an adult I became troubled by what seemed like a nervous habit: I would chew on the lower right side of my lip when anxious or under stress. During one of my therapy sessions, I slowed down this movement and brought awareness to its inner impulse, and I was able to make the emotional connection with my grief over the losses of Aunt Sunshe and Grandpa Max, and thus release that repetitive motor habit. I then found myself able to cry more freely.* At first I accomplished this by rereading books from my childhood, especially adventure books for kids around the age I had been when I served as a pallbearer, books like Mark Twain's *Tom Sawyer* and *Huckleberry Finn*. I also watched emotionally poignant films. These, in turn, helped me to gradually open to the grief of my abandoned inner child. I was then better able to reclaim this hurt child with love and self-compassion, and with tears of relief.

---

*One of my students suggested I watch a particular interview with Prince Harry. During the interview, it was clear he was also biting his lip when he talked about his grief over his mother's death.

Tears in Blood

As a means to allow greater vulnerability and deeper intimate connection, I continued to search for and surrender to my tears. I recall a very important opening in this regard. It happened in 1967 when I was with my Berkeley girlfriend, Ellie. She was a singer—a "hot lick"—in a cool folk, jazz, country, swing, bluegrass, and gypsy band called Dan Hicks and the Hot Licks. There were many occasions when they opened at the Fillmore West in San Francisco for the likes of Janis Joplin, Jefferson Airplane, the Grateful Dead, and Canned Heat, to mention just a few rock headliners. As you can imagine, there were drugs and booze galore.

One day Ellie and I went to her father's Mendocino ranch. We decided to drop LSD. As we walked into the forest, I was overcome by immobilizing dread and despair. Somehow I knew to ask Ellie to hold me. I then hallucinated the image of a tear, which filled with bright red blood. Within the tear and blood emerged a pulsing, beating heart. My tears welled up and I quietly sobbed for an hour in Ellie's holding arms. It seemed the frozen shock from my mother's stifling gaze had been melted. As we continued on our walk, everything in the forest, especially the ferns, became intensely alive. As did I.

I later reflected on this image with a close friend. It became clear that the blood filling the tear, and the beating heart, were about releasing my held-in grief. But more than that, the blood and beating heart symbolized the recapturing of my vitality, my life force. However, had I not been able to surrender to Ellie's holding embrace, it is likely this would have been a "bad trip" taking me into endless terror.

The Last Shaman

I have frequently been asked my opinion about the use of psychedelics and hallucinogens in therapy. Having come of age at Berkeley in the 1960s, I most certainly dabbled with pot, LSD, and other hallucinogens. In the 1970s I was introduced to MDMA, originally called ADAM and known much later as the party drug ecstasy. I also sampled MDA, a more powerful analogue of MDMA. Both these drugs were fully legal in the 1970s and were synthesized by a wild, hip Bay Area chemist named Sasha Shulgin. Around this time a Berkeley psychiatrist named Leo Zeff began conducting therapy sessions for couples in which he administered MDMA to dissolve their defensiveness, to help them contact their inner truths, and to open their hearts and communicate honestly with each other. Finally, a small group of us utilized MDMA to assist in psychotherapy, as a way to help individuals take a compassionate distance from their wounds and traumas, so they might better observe, process, and heal.

These encounters helped me to develop Somatic Experiencing, the body-oriented approach in which I have been able to help my clients achieve many of these benefits without the use of psychedelics. But I have observed there could be a great benefit from a synergistic relationship between both approaches, particularly by preparing for the psychedelic journey with cleansing practices and intentions, as well as following up afterward with review and integration with body sensations.

The importance of preparation has been poignantly demonstrated in the *The Last Shaman*, a film that touched me deeply. This documentary is about a young man suffering from chronic depression. He tries medication after medication and even subjects himself to ECT, or Electroconvulsive Therapy, previously known as Electric Convulsive Shock Treatment. Both his professional parents, while caring for his financial and academic welfare, were clearly lacking in their capacity to meet his basic human needs as an infant and young child. They failed to provide him with bonding, physical contact, mirroring, and emotional warmth. In some ways I could identify with his plight. In this film, the young man goes desperately searching the Peruvian highlands to find a shaman and to receive ayahuasca, a powerful plant-based psychedelic. However, encountering shaman after shaman, he is gravely disappointed by their greed for money and power. He witnesses how some of them use their charisma to manipulate and exert control over seekers, all to feed their egos and hunger for power. But, finally, the young man meets Pepe, a more authentic shaman, in a remote mountain village. The healer takes the boy under his wing and advises him of certain daily rituals he must practice for a month. Only after doing so will he be able to take the psychedelic journey with the shaman.

As the young man diligently employs these rituals, we see him bond with the warm families of the village, especially their children. When he is finally given the ayahuasca, one sees how these simple mountain people have provided him with comfort and compassion and thus have greatly impacted his transformation. In fact, this gentle atmosphere was likely as important as the daily preparation rituals. I believe it was the combination of the ayahuasca, the ritual practices, and the warmth and stability of his adopted village support system that helped lighten his burden of depression. This depression was a deep anguish derived from the empty, cold, and emotionally vacant home environment of his childhood. With this weight lifted at last, he could find a way forward in his life.

There is great promise in the use of psychedelic substances for healing, yet there are also potential pitfalls that need to be fully and openly examined. This critical consideration can be difficult, as one sometimes sees an almost messianic and sometimes naive embrace of these substances as a panacea. In contrast to my laissez-faire and freewheeling attitude of the 1960s and 1970s regarding the use of these substances therapeutically, my current perspective is more thoughtful, measured, and, embarrassingly, perhaps more "conservative." To quote the poignant Joni Mitchell song, first recorded by Judy Collins, *I've looked at clouds from both sides now.**

In pursuit of a more balanced view, it is useful to deconstruct the young man's experience with the shaman and the village community and see how it might serve as a framework for the therapeutic use of these powerful substances. We might first look to the intention and preparation of the young man as he searched for healing and for the right shaman, or in other words, a guide well versed in understanding the benefits and risks of a particular substance, when to use it and in what dosages, and how to follow-up. Of greatest importance is that, like the "Last Shaman" Pepe, the integrity of the guide or therapist must be firmly established by trusted referral sources, and by sincere and clear communication between the seeker and the therapist. Only then should any of these catalysts be used, with the right guide, a stable environment, and the all-important follow-up. Care is needed to integrate the experience and ground it in the felt-body.

In addition to facilitating work with specific traumas, psychedelics can also be valuable when people, like the young man, are suffering from an "endogenous" depression due to lack of emotional

---

*I do not advise anyone to try psychedelics without careful preparation, and then only with an experienced and knowledgeable guide and with adequate follow-up.

warmth, support, and reflection. This is in part because psychedelics can help individuals open to the transcendent function—a term used by Carl G. Jung to describe spiritual individuation. So while we cannot change the fact that we did not receive warmth and affection from our parents and caregivers, we can still open to the transcendent. For me this nurturing presence was embodied in the archetypal image of the Black Madonna. A similar transformative state can also be facilitated by a number of other substances, particularly a drug called 5-MeO-DMT. An advantage of this substance is its relatively short duration of action, about thirty to forty-five minutes for the most intense period, after which it takes the client an additional two or three hours to return to their usual state of mind and to take note of what comes up during that integration phase. Because these types of substances are tremendously potent and send the individual into such an extraordinary reality, they require a high level of preparation and follow-up with a therapist familiar not only with the particular substance but also how to integrate the experience in one's body. There is a saying from Papua New Guinea: "Knowledge is useless until it lives in the body." And so this is true for "experienced knowledge" (*gnosis*) gained from psychedelics and grounding it in the body, in the here and now.

In review: Having first found the right guide, one should consider, secondly, how to ready oneself for a journey of this nature. In the documentary the young man is required to engage in preparation rituals for a specific period of time. A third precondition we must meet is to have a supportive environment, as was offered by the warm-hearted villagers. And finally, a fourth element must be to allow time for rest, review, and integration of the experience before re-engaging in one's previous everyday life.

It is also important to have continuing support as one assimilates what might emerge in the aftermath of psychedelic use. This can include continued contact with the therapist or guide, as well as time spent in meditation or other body-based awareness pathways, so we can touch elements of the stimulating drug episode over time. It is important to recapture and engage various sensations, feelings, images, and memories while also assimilating these various altered states of consciousness (ASC). I believe that, in general, for every psychedelic session there should be at least ten to fifteen follow-up therapy sessions without the psychedelic substance—including sessions that are preparatory, or before substance use, and integrative, or after use.

For preparation, I would suggest the client complete a two- or three-hour session without the drug, wearing an eye mask and headphones with music playing. The task of the therapist is then to observe and work with whatever memories, emotions, or sensations come up for the individual. Essentially this is preconditioning for how the later drug episode will be orchestrated over several hours. This way the person becomes familiar with how the session might go, learning what comes up and if they feel comfortable and safe enough to complete the later session with the catalyst. About a week after the appointment using the drug, I would recommend the individual do a follow-up session, again with the music and eye mask, and be tracked by the therapist for as many hours as needed.

One of the potentially significant pitfalls of these powerful medicines is the danger in unsupervised use. I was clearly fortunate to have things go the way they did during my LSD "trip," which led me to deep, heartfelt healing, and not to severe re-traumatization. This was sheer luck, however, which speaks to the risk of undergoing these journeys outside a controlled therapeutic milieu. Indeed, sometimes the temptation to ingest one of these substances can be very strong, particularly when a person is re-experiencing depression, anxiety, or the emergence of traumatic memories and sensations. Since some of these substances can be found "on the street" or even over the internet, one must prepare clients to seek council and support when they are struggling with these issues, and ensure they have the opportunity to meet with their therapist, or the impulsive search for relief could end in disaster—as it could have for me without the fortuitous, vital support of Ellie.*

To close this section, I would like to honor the pioneers in the field of psychedelic therapy. First, for hundreds of years, shamans throughout the world have used various plant and other natural substances to treat what South American healers called "Susto," which translates to "fright paralysis," a sudden feeling of fear or dread—in other words, trauma!

The grandfather of synthesized psychedelic agents was the Swiss chemist Albert Hofmann, who, while working at the Sandoz Laboratories in Basel, Switzerland, "accidently" discovered LSD-25. He then communicated the effects of this substance to Dr. Humphry Osmond, who in the 1950s was working at Weyburn Mental Hospital in the boondocks of Saskatchewan, Canada. Osmond realized that people who would otherwise have languished for years in mental asylums could get their lives back using LSD. It was Osmond, incidentally, who coined the word "psychedelics."

In mid-1950s Stanislav Grof, a pioneer in LSD research, began his seminal work. He was a Czechoslovakian-born psychiatrist working at the Spring Grove Hospital in Catonsville, Maryland.

---

*On a very positive note, a nonprofit organization called the Multidisciplinary Association for Psychedelic Studies (MAPS) currently conducts and promotes psychedelic research worldwide, including at some of the most prestigious university medical schools.

Grof conducted extensive research on psychedelic therapy with psychiatric patients. As part of this research, he had patients record their therapy by creating remarkable drawings and paintings. One day, at the Esalen Institute in Big Sur, California, where we were both teaching workshops, I spoke to Grof about his research life. He reflected that in Communist Czechoslovakia, he had intellectual and professional freedom but little personal freedom. But, he bemoaned, when he immigrated to the United States he had personal freedom but much less professional freedom; indeed, his research was curtailed and remained dormant for many decades.

Fast forward to the present day and it is remarkable how much the field has changed for the better, and that these substances will be used responsibly and efficaciously.

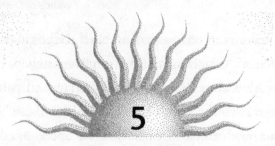

5

Wounds of Betrayal

I understand pain. I've lived with pain my entire life.
But pain is nothing compared to betrayal.
And betrayal is nothing compared to knowing that
the javelin in your back was rammed there
by the one person in your life you actually trusted.

BRAD MELTZER, *THE BOOK OF LIES*

At around the age of eight, my uncle Jack (my mother's younger brother and a very important figure in my life) took me to an electrical warehouse owned by a cousin. As we walked together along the narrow aisles of the warehouse, my eyes fixed upon a bin of electric house buzzers and push-button switches. I made a point of returning to that aisle alone, then held my breath in anticipation as I furtively grabbed both a buzzer and a push button and stuffed them into my bulging pants pocket. My heart raced in my throat. Fearing I would be caught, I remained in a state of anxious expectancy until we reached my family's Bronx apartment. Once there, I rushed down to the basement where I commandeered a large cardboard box that had previously housed a brand-new, 1940s-era television set.

I hurried upstairs to our apartment with the empty box securely cradled in my arms. Grabbing a knife from the kitchen, I cut a door and a little window into the box. I then fastened the precious new button and buzzer to the door of my "secret clubhouse." After connecting the buzzer to an electrical socket, I was delighted to hear its loud, raspy buzzing and was particularly buoyed by the notion that any visitor would have to push the button and ring the buzzer to get permission to enter my private hideout, my sanctuary of safety and refuge. This was a way of protecting myself by setting and maintaining a safe and audible protective boundary.*

My parents must have heard the loud buzzing and figured from whence it came. I imagine they quickly guessed I'd snuck the items out of the store. Together they rushed into my bedroom, grabbed my arms, and pulled me from my once-secure haven. Dragging me down the hallway and into the living room, they hurled a volley of rapid-fire questions and accusations at me, to which I responded with pleading denials. Then, one after the other, they took turns slapping my face as they shoved me back and forth between them. Their Stasi-style interrogation went on for several minutes, but it seemed forever. I finally broke down in wrenching sobs and confessed to my crime. My spirit was shattered. Defeated, I slunk off to my bed, and with muted cries I fell into an agitated sleep. When I awoke, it was to a different world.

I know of many individuals, both personally and professionally, who endured childhoods replete with ongoing violence, abuse, and neglect. In comparison I feel the violence and abuse I bore doesn't compare to theirs. But having worked with traumatized people for

---

*I was rather lucky I didn't electrocute myself, because as I later found out, the buzzer was meant to operate on a 24-volt transformer, not a 120-volt electric socket!

nearly half a century, I believe it is a misstep to compare traumas. If I have learned anything, it is that trauma is trauma, no matter the source! So while ongoing violence and abuse lead to emotional constriction, dissociation, and physical pain, betrayal has the additional insult of being an injury by the very person or people we have trusted to care for, love, and protect us. After such a betrayal it seems as if nothing about the world makes sense.

Before this betrayal, when I was around the age of seven, I built a crystal radio set by myself. Well, not entirely—I did receive help from my mother. We had taken a mailing tube, wound a wire coil around it, and somehow found a small piece of germanium crystal and fastened a "cat's whisker" from a bent safety pin. A friend of my grandfather's had given me a World War II–era headset to use with the makeshift radio. Finally, we stretched a wire out one of our windows to fashion an antenna. After dangling the aerial wire out the window, we breathlessly tuned the coil and then could barely, and only at night, pick up one faint radio station, CBS. I was then forever possessed by an avid fascination with electricity and electrical devices, marking the start of a burgeoning calling to science and electronics.

In spite of the association with electronics and emotional pain, this calling was a generous gift that my mother afforded me. Some years later, as a thirteen-year-old, this enthusiasm led me to become an amateur shortwave "Ham" radio operator. It was thrilling to send and receive Morse code. In this way I came to communicate, in dots and dashes, with fellow Ham operators all over the globe. This contact opened a grand new world for me. At one point, after many hours of practice, I was able to send and receive over fifty words per minute in Morse code. This made me eligible to sit for an exam in electronics and shortwave regulations. I then received my advanced radio license at the ripe old age of fourteen. This certification allowed me to use voice as well as Morse code to communicate. Remember, this was half a century before the popularization of cell phones and the internet!

With soldering iron and needle-nose pliers in hand, I built a shortwave receiver and transmitter from kits manufactured by the Heath Company in Benton Harbor, Michigan, the go-to source for young Hams on a limited budget. These kits engaged my full attention and tested the boundaries of my technical skills. As I look back on the excitement and passion I poured into these projects, I believe my earlier efforts in building the crystal set with my mother at age seven gave me the impetus to take on this complex task at fourteen. It was also a way to distract myself from the rape, as well as the ongoing threat of the mafia, my father's looming incarceration, and the parental betrayal.

My Ham call letters were K2VTL. When I spoke over the airwaves, I identified myself with these call letters: "King 2 Victor Thomas Love." Later I got creative, using a few adroit phonetics: "This is K2 Very Tough Luck." Or, "This is K2VTL, Kiss Two Very Tender Lips." In reflection, this was also a time of my difficult sexual awakening—more on this later.

Many nights I would stay up late and quietly turn on my receiver and transmitter. I would don my headphones and switch on a microphone, which was improperly grounded so occasionally gave me a small shock. Anyhow, I was ready to go! This nocturnal venture took advantage of the ionospheric bounce, which is much better at night, and facilitated my talking to people over the whole globe. In this way I learned to decipher foreign accents and found out a little about these strangers' lives. Now, sixty-five years later, while teaching Somatic Experiencing in many countries, I am at ease listening to a variety of students' accents and encountering their wondrous cultural differences. I have been able to learn a few words in other languages, and even occasionally a few sentences. And as a teacher, I have again been able to communicate with the world.

Returning to the violent interrogation and betrayal by my parents—this hardened my young heart. Thereafter I somehow knew I deserved to be punished; that I was, at heart, a bad person and a criminal. Later as an adult, I lived with the persistent fear that I would be exposed as a fraud and an imposter. It seemed I was forever condemned to wear this branding. That label has followed me for much of my life, and it took some years of diligent inner work to shed this disabling self-perception, one that had long thwarted my ability to be successful and achieve what I yearned for in my life.

After great reflection, and by developing self-compassion, I came to understand that the missing words my "good enough" parents might have said were: "Peter, it's amazing you were able to connect the buzzer and make it work. But it's not okay to have taken it without asking. We will go back to the store, and you can buy the buzzer and apologize for taking it. And Peter, had you asked us, we would have been glad to buy it for you! You just need to ask." This is what my adult self would say to such an errant child. And these were the very words that emerged from a therapy session in which an image of Albert Einstein spontaneously appeared. He talked to my parents, speaking firmly yet compassionately to them, and said those supportive, healing words to me—yet another indication Einstein was my guide and protector.

In my early forties I went to visit my parents and asked them if they remembered this violent episode. "No," my father said firmly, "that never happened." Yet even as he spoke, my mother's eyes welled up with deep sadness, and she interrupted him: "No, Morris, it really did happen. We were scared; we never should have done that.

It was wrong, it was hurtful—we really hurt him. We were wrong." Though many decades had passed since that frightening day, it was still somehow relieving to hear her belated acknowledgment of the event and her sincere admission of the abuse it entailed. Such is the value of emotional healing as I now understand it.

As painful as this injury was, I later discovered that this incident was only the second significant betrayal in my young life. The initial wounding was much deeper and more injurious. It occurred when I was barely six months old. And it became my core injury and primal betrayal. This was a rupture that undermined my resilience and left me with a shaky foundation on which to build. Later betrayals and wounds would only add to this underlying fragility and anxious attachment to my parents.

This event occurred in 1942, as the United States was readying to enter World War II. My parents were worried my father would be drafted to fight in Europe. With this looming uncertainty, they made the hasty decision to take a vacation together for three weeks. Abruptly, they deposited me with my maternal grandparents who, though kind, were near-strangers to me. There are no words to describe the utterly devastating effect of such an early separation and abandonment.

In a psychology "experiment" on child development, a young child was brought into a strange room by its mother and left there with an unknown female researcher. At first the baby cried inconsolably, and then screamed in paroxysms of rage. He could not be soothed by the female researcher, despite her gentle ministrations. After a short while, the young child collapsed into what seemed a state of shutdown and helpless resignation. There he remained, mute and immobile, and would only play alone with some toy blocks. In a few minutes when the mother returned, the baby appeared not to recognize her. He just stared blankly into space. There was little in the way of the necessary reunion, even when she reached to pick him up.

When I first saw this video, I was horrified. I could see the monumental effect this brief episode of sudden separation had on the small child. These few minutes must have seemed an eternity to a baby. I suspect my concern was also an unconscious reaction to my own three-week abandonment. I was particularly worried about any lasting effect this separation might have had on the baby—and upon me! Indeed, some years later, the same child—now a toddler—was brought back to the room from the earlier experiment. Though safe in its mother's arms this time, the youngster showed signs of distress and agitation. Clearly the effect of those few minutes of separation was long-lasting and possibly substantial. How, then, would three weeks of abandonment affect a baby—a baby who was not even securely attached to begin with? The answer: utter and complete annihilation! My own eventual recall of such obliteration was nothing even faintly resembling a conscious memory. It was, rather, an abandonment crisis lodged deep in my psyche and stored as a "body memory," one that would take much diligent work, along with an occasional synchronicity, to unearth and dislodge. To illustrate this, I offer the following example.

During a visit to my parents about thirty years ago, my mother, unannounced, put her arm around my shoulders. I stiffened and asked her to take her arm away. Sometime after this, I requested the help of one of my trainees to address this fear that came up with my mother, and which was likely being played out in a line of fractured relationships. The fear manifested as a wrenching in my gut and a heavy sinking in my belly. I felt panic and sheer dread, as though I couldn't catch my breath. With my trainee's calm guidance, I gradually was able to steady my breath—and then felt an abrupt stiffness in my arms. In further exploration it seemed both my arms were bracing, holding back an impending doom. I felt as if I would be completely annihilated. There are no words to fully describe this devastation. It was sheer obliteration and terror.

I had no context for this terror and the stiffening of my arms. It felt as though, if I let go of that tension, I would somehow be ripped open. My next step was to speak to my mother again, and I was able to open my heart to her. She seemed on the verge of tears as she told me that after that three-week separation, every time she took me to visit my grandparents, I would frantically brace with my arms against entering their apartment. My hands would seize the entrance doorframe as I screamed bloody murder. Both my mother and I knew just what that meant—and it must have been horribly difficult for her to reckon with how terrifying and long-lasting this wound of abandonment was for me. I think she felt horribly guilty for having inflicted this enduring torment.*

To try to make sense of such a betrayal, we may split the offending parent into two different versions: one that is nurturing, supportive, and safe, and one that is dangerous. We are then faced with the plaguing question of how to hold the pieces of this seismic fracture together, without falling apart ourselves. Such a balancing act is, at best, a daunting task. In reality most of our parents have a mixture of both good and bad qualities. For growth to occur, we must learn to weave these two opposites into a coherent narrative, and thus make sense of our journey through life. In my case, this

---

*Indeed, I later used a variety of psychedelics to further dislodge this frozen horror and panic, so deep and mortal was the injury.

splitting may have played out through a tendency to mentally label my relationships as either "all good" or "all bad." Not a viable or realistic solution, to say the least!

In reflecting upon how this primal abandonment undermined my adult relationships, I realized I would often feel an inexplicable panic when a girlfriend seemed to withdraw from me. Sometimes I would sabotage a relationship by abruptly pulling away before a partner could abandon me. Or, conversely, I would stay in a relationship too long—perhaps due to my fear of being alone. I have sometimes struggled with uncertainty over why I wanted to end a relationship. Was I doing so to protect myself from being abandoned, or was it honestly the right time to end it? And how could I tell the difference? To this question, I am reminded of the Serenity Prayer, which goes like this: "God, grant me the serenity to accept the things I cannot change, the courage to change the things I can, and the wisdom to know the difference." And it is that courage and wisdom that I strive to bring into my life. My deepest hope for any relationship is that much is learned about love, respect, healthy boundaries, and freely given kindness, no matter whether one chooses to stay or to leave.

With much gratitude to past partners, and with the goal of establishing and maintaining enduring, healthy relationships, I am now learning to generate my own internal well-being. This transformation has been accompanied by feelings of joy and even spontaneous outbursts of laughter. I have felt an inner shift as a result of the gentle desire to share these precious moments with others. With that aim in mind, I recall a song by the Eagles that speaks to such internal growth and grounding. The song goes like this: *And I got a peaceful, easy feelin' / And I know you won't let me down / 'Cause I'm already standin' on the ground.* Though it has been a long and circuitous journey, I now feel that I mostly have my feet on the ground, and I am embarking on a grand journey of relationship to self and others. Through that dual task, I am learning to more fully inhabit my living, sensing, knowing body. As in the song, I don't have that panicky feeling of being let down, "'Cause I'm already standing on the ground."

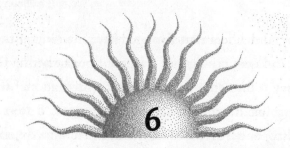

6

Pouncer the Dingo Dog

J'ai suivi une femme (I followed a woman)
et j'ai trouvé un chien (and I found a dog)

In 1978 when I was in my early thirties, I was teaching at the Esalen Institute in the wilds of Big Sur, California. I walked into a room where there was an ongoing presentation of a type of bodywork. While Arthur Pauls explained his method, called Ortho-Bionomy, a young woman demonstrated the technique on a man lying on a massage table. She was clearly a natural healer and carried herself gracefully. I was quickly overtaken by her regal presence, and truth be told, I fell immediately under her spell.

Though shy and reluctant, I worked up the courage to approach her. After an awkward introduction, I was relieved and then bashfully thrilled when she offered me her phone number and agreed to a rendezvous in Berkeley. Her name was Erika. We began casually getting together in spite of the informal nature of our meeting. However, my enchantment was rudely shaken and I fell back to earth when I encountered the cold reality of her unsatisfying job and shady circle. It turned out Erika was working as a parts runner for a motorcycle shop. Her boyfriend at the time was a champion drag racer and deliberately sabotaged her emerging gifts as a healer. As we got to know each other, I learned her father had abandoned her as a very young child, along with her disabled brother and her struggling single mom. The family had not heard from him since. But, as it happened, even before the internet we were able to locate her father, who now lived in Phoenix, Arizona.

Besides becoming her lover and friend, I became a witness to her vast potential as a healer and would eventually encourage her to study physical therapy, where she clearly excelled. In order to follow her dream, she decided to move to Flagstaff, Arizona, where she could attend the physical therapy program at Northern Arizona University. She later graduated cum laude.

After several months of intermittent visits, I decided to follow her there. I packed up my house, closed my therapy practice in Berkeley, and headed south. For a city boy, moving off to a frontier mountain town was a true adventure. However, when Erika arrived in Flagstaff, she met a neighbor who was similar to the motorcycle friends she'd left behind in a Richmond ghetto. She was attracted to him, as she had been with her Bay Area racing-car crowd. In reflection, I believe she couldn't tolerate having both her aspirations realized simultaneously: being accepted into physical therapy school and having me move to Arizona to be with her. She needed to fall back on what was familiar, at least in one area of her life. And after junior college, she seemed to recognize the importance of giving herself the education and vocation of her dreams. Thankfully, she was to succeed in that endeavor.

When I saw Erika with her neighbor, all was clear to me— they were seeing each other romantically. I was utterly devastated. Brokenhearted, I hunkered down in my house, which was at the edge of the forest. One day I walked into these woods and came across the Coconino Humane Association. I entered the building and walked among the cages. I was struck by one particular puppy, who I later learned was a Dingo–Australian Shepherd mix. Interestingly, according to Australian Aboriginal lore, the Dingo is sacred and known as the intermediary between the physical and spiritual realms. This canine "avatar" would become my best and most trusted friend. As our eyes met, I felt we were supposed to be together. At the risk of sounding too New Age, I believe we were communicating not just in the tangible world but also on a metaphysical level.

I asked the man working at the shelter if I could take the dog out behind the center in a heavily wooded area. He agreed. Incredibly, the puppy walked by my side, nearly touching me, as though I had taught him to heel—which obviously I hadn't. Every time I stopped, he stopped. Every time I sat down, he would sit down next to me. Another exceptional quality I witnessed as we walked in the woods: he would enthusiastically jump up and pounce, reminding me of dolphins surfing the ocean waves; hence, he became known as "Pouncer."

From that time on, we developed an extraordinary bond, one that would help me heal from the betrayal wound left by Erika and move forward in my life. It was a bond of a kind that was wholly new to me. Simply put, I received my kindergarten lessons about joy, attachment, and love from Pouncer the Dingo, an intermediating link between the worlds.

I have several stories that speak to Pouncer's emotional and cognitive intelligence. Pouncer had one particular habit that required stern commands on my part. While he was free to chase wild rabbits, I was concerned about his penchant for chasing deer into the mountain hills behind my house. So, at the moment his body stiffened in readiness, I would sternly (but gently) command him with, "No, Pouncer!" This was the first and nearly the last time I had to set such a definitive boundary with him. The second boundary was about bedtime. I didn't want us to sleep together, so his bed was in the living room near my bedroom. However, this did not deter me from joining him on the floor for some jovial rough-and-tumble play, warm hugs, and soothing touches.

I don't know how, but he learned not to enter my bedroom in the morning until I had opened my eyes. He would then gently knock on the door with his paws, and I would let him in. He bounded into the room with unbridled enthusiasm and joy at the prospect of starting the day together. How he knew this timing always puzzled me. But such was the nature of our mysterious, unspoken communication.

However, on one occasion he didn't adhere to these unwritten rules. In the middle of the night I awoke to hear him frantically scratching at my door. I opened it in exasperation and scolded him with my eyes. He ignored my reaction, bolted into the room, and cowered in a corner. It was then that I caught the unmistakable scent of a black bear. Immediately I too backed into the room, closed the door, and fetched my .45-caliber revolver, just in case the bear charged and attacked me. I crept down the hall toward the racket in the kitchen; the entire floor was covered with flour and other dry staples. I tried to coax the bear out the now-broken dog door through which it had entered. However, this was to no avail: she just stared at me. I picked up a pot and pan and banged them together. Still no reaction. So I grabbed the biggest pot and biggest pan and banged those wildly together. To my surprise both handles broke off, and the pieces of the pot and pan flew overhead and clattered to the floor in front of the spooked bear. She summarily lumbered toward the broken dog door. Relieved, Pouncer came slinking out from his hiding place, and we joyfully celebrated our victory together. I quickly boarded up the bashed-in door, and we slept together for this one night before returning to our separate sleeping quarters.

A final poignant episode with Pouncer still fills me with fond gladness. When I lived in western Nevada, during the winter I would frequently go skiing, either downhill or cross country. When I chose downhill, Pouncer would have to wait in my truck, and every hour or so I would let him run around the parking lot. However, when I went cross-country skiing, Pouncer was like a snow dolphin, leaping in joyful arcs by my side.

At the end of a week of powder snowfall, I excitedly went into the basement of my house and collected my downhill boots. When I returned with my skis, Pouncer seemed despondent, lying still with paws over his head. But then in a flash he perked up, ran down into the basement, and returned with a cross-country ski boot in his mouth. "Okay, Pouncer, you win," I said as I went downstairs into the basement one more time and returned with the second cross-country boot, along with my Nordic skis. We were off to a glorious day of cross-country skiing, Pouncer dolphining through the powder, close by my side, always perfectly aligned, always in easy resonance. Our friendship was passionate and deeply nourishing. He touched my life, and I am forever changed by this spirit of comradery.

When I watched my recordings of client sessions, especially those with children, I would often see Pouncer circling around the child. He would then sit down quietly by their side. In one particular session, I was treating a twelve-year-old boy whose best friend, a child who had lived next door to him, was murdered late one night.

My client, who I will call Eric, felt enormously guilty and believed he should have been able to save his friend. Even though this was irrational, Eric couldn't untangle his guilt from his grief for his lost friend. His sleep was greatly disturbed, and he was paralyzed with self-blame. He was unable to return to school because of his crippling anxiety. In one of our final sessions, I made a cave out of a couple of folded futons. Eric crawled in, followed by Pouncer and me. I observed, breathlessly, as Pouncer gently licked and touched his nose to a small scar on Eric's cheek. Eric then began to sob deeply and fully, while he let me and Pouncer hold and rock him.

Eric told me about a haunting dream he had on the night of the murder. Remarkably, he reported he had dreamt that the intruder had broken into his friend's house and was going to kill his friend. This was, likely, his survivor's guilt being playing out. Together, as we talked, Eric, Pouncer, and I recognized that the dream had actually occurred two nights *after* the murder. This discovery allowed Eric to fully face his grief over losing his best friend, and gently released him from his paralyzing guilt. We also learned from his mother that the small scar on his cheek, exactly where Pouncer had "kissed" him, was where a dog had bitten him when he was four years old.

Pouncer's primal empathy broke through Eric's terror and confusion. A terror that came from the four-year-old child's trauma with an attacking dog, and now, eight years later, with a friend's violent death. The ensuing tears seem to wash away much of his pain and school anxiety. Eric could sleep soundly once again, per his mother's follow-up report. From then on, he returned to his former engagement with school and his classmates.

After my session with Eric, I began seeing other children at my house on Apple Valley Road in Lyons, Colorado. There we would pack sandwiches and snacks, and together with Pouncer, we would head into the mountains behind my home. When I was with traumatized, depressed, or anxious kids, Pouncer would run circles around them until the child became engaged. They would play together with laughter and spirited barking. The child would often throw sticks, and Pouncer would leap in the air, pounce on the prized object before retrieving it, and then gleefully return it to the thrilled child. It was a scene of irresistible delight and joyful exuberance, a sure remedy for a distressed child. Pouncer had a sixth sense for how to reach into their troubled hearts and entice them out of their lonely caves of despair.

Pouncer taught me to trust my deep intuition. He gave me a firsthand lesson in how to spontaneously engage with respect, love, joy, and above all with play. He offered this play as the medium for his unfiltered emotional or sensate intelligence. If my mind would try to figure out what to do, it was far less effective than what his animal instinct understood was needed. I am so thankful to Pouncer for teaching me to follow my gut and my heart.

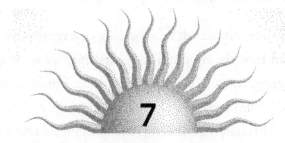

7

A Sexual Awakening, Delayed

Writing this chapter has been the greatest challenge for me. It holds my most hidden and deeply vulnerable truths. However in setting them down here, I have tried to be patient with myself, just as I hope you will offer yourself the same leniency.

I once asked a group of therapists if they ever brought up sexual issues in sessions. Out of a few hundred, only one or two raised their hands. I then inquired how many of their clients brought these issues into therapy. A small number raised their hands. Finally, I asked how they might proceed if a client did bring up sexual concerns. In response, I got two answers. One was to direct the therapy session toward a discussion of attachment issues, and the other was to refer the client to a sex therapist. While these might be good options, we often miss the salient questions of how the client inhabits their body, and of how they live—their life force, their life energy, and thus healthy sexuality. Issues related to sex are not usually about the mechanics of their "plumbing," or about increasing their arousal cycles. Rather the question is how they share their warmth, deep feelings, vitality, excitement, and sensuality with a chosen other. This way it becomes a celebration and deep connection. By including this chapter and opening up about my struggles, as difficult as they were, I hope to help others in their own sexual healing.

I can readily relate to the reluctance to put oneself out there, as sexuality is a tremendously delicate and sensitive subject. However, it is one that often needs to be addressed with our clients, and ourselves, to help them have a truly robust and healthy relationship to themselves and to their chosen other. So, with this in mind, I have decided to tenderly reveal some of my own sexual healing and erotic maturation process.

When I was about five years old, my mother would often read to me at bedtime. This was the closest and most intimate exchange we shared. One night, as we lay under the covers together, she read to me from my favorite book, *Huckleberry Finn*. In my joy and excitement, I had a sudden erection, a fairly normal occurrence for a healthy five-year-old. My mother immediately closed the book and stood up abruptly, leaving my bedroom without a word and quickly closing the door behind her. Not one word was said about this occurrence. However, the message was clear: I can have *either* physical and emotional closeness *or* awaken to my sexual feelings, but not both. This was a split that would follow me through much of my adult life. Her repressed erotic legacy would become my healing challenge.

I am not sure whether this was a coincidence, but my mother seemed to become afraid to read to me. I recall that from this time forward my father was the parent who read to me in bed. What I remember the most is how he would sometimes sing to me. There are two songs that remain most vivid in my mind. The first was "On the Road to Mandalay" by Rudyard Kipling, written in 1890: *On the road to Mandalay, / Where the flyin'-fishes play, / An' the dawn comes up like thunder outer China 'crost the Bay!*

And then my father would clap his hands together and make the sound of thunder, . . . which both scared and thrilled me. The second song was the French childhood classic: *Frère Jacques, Frère Jacques. Dormez-vous? Dormez-vous? Sonnez les matines! Sonnez les matines! Ding, dong, ding. Ding, dong, ding.*

I loved these interludes, and I would have him sing them to me, again and again. He could tell that I was fascinated by the French, so he would then talk to me in what was fluent French. When I first went to France in the 1970s, I was surprised at how familiar that language seemed to me, and so much so that I could readily pick up some of these words and sentences. See plate 4 for a photo of my father in his youth.

Barry

The next occurrence in my sequence of stifled Eros happened in my early adolescence.

My friends and I liked to play stickball, a "pick-up" street game similar to baseball, except that it was played with a broomstick. This alteration was due to the general poverty of our neighborhood, where kids couldn't afford a real bat, a baseball, and gloves. Instead, the equipment consisted of a broom handle and a rubber ball, typically a fifteen-cent Spaldeen or Pensy Pinky. In doing a little research, I learned that a variant of the stickball game actually dates back to the 1750s!

Because I was an awkward, skinny kid, I was always picked last when we chose teams. Therefore, whenever I engaged in these pick-up games, I couldn't shake off a persistent undercurrent of inferiority and humiliation. In contrast, Barry Goldberg—the only other Jewish kid, and a red-haired one at that—was the star athlete. He was always the first team member to be picked after we flipped a coin. I don't remember exactly how it came about, but Barry and I formed a friendship. We would meet up after school to play and engage in athletic activities. After a while, I seemed to absorb some of his skill. When we would run around the track in the park, below where I was later raped, I could almost catch up to him; I would feel power surging through my legs. And when we practiced broad jumping in a sawdust pit, I was once again nearly his equal. From then on, when the gang played stickball, I was usually picked second or third, instead of last. My life felt as though it was turning around.

Barry and I became best friends, and with this bonding, we began to explore masturbation—enhanced by the *Playboy* magazine's nude centerfolds. We also shared a filial, though forbidden, attraction. As these sexual interests grew, we decided to try mutual masturbation while locked inside my tiny bathroom. But during this timid early exploration, we were interrupted by a loud banging on the door! We froze in abject horror as my father shouted, "If you and Barry are doing something in there, then he can't ever come back here and be your friend!"

I felt as if I'd been gut punched. I was totally breathless; time seemed to have frozen. I can still feel some residue of that distressing memory, even in writing these words today. It was like I lost my best friend in one moment, all because of this erotic affection and experimentation. With Barry, I could either have an open and chaste friendship or a hidden adolescent exploration, but never both. Looking back, I am pretty sure that, had things been allowed to run their course, we would have naturally grown out of it.

Yet my excitement and arousal had been shattered and radically shamed, echoing my mother's rejection of my sexuality with her abrupt departure when I was five. Once again, I could not enjoy emotional connection *and* be a sexual being. I had to choose. I was devastated, and my emerging sexuality was driven deep underground, where it languished for some decades.

Gratitude

My disastrous first sexual encounter was with Joanne, whom I met with my Beatnik friends in the back room of the Michigan student union. She rather quickly invited me to her off-campus apartment. There, in a darkened room filled only with colored light bulbs and candles, she seduced me. As she pulled me inside her, I immediately ejaculated. Bummer! The next day, as I walked to the campus from her apartment, I wondered if the people I met on the street could tell that I was no longer a virgin.

But things got much worse. I moved in with Joanne and realized she was a junkie, addicted to morphine and especially methamphetamine. I innocently thought I would rescue her and she would stop. Today I feel embarrassed even acknowledging my own naïveté. Finally the amphetamines caused her to have some kind of psychotic episode, during which she broke windows and was probably in an acutely paranoid state. I called the hospital and she was picked up by an ambulance. I was beside myself with worry. Apparently the psychiatrist, a first-year resident and obviously a budding Freudian, told her that her addiction was "because she wanted to have her father's penis." But I would guess her amphetamine use started when she was failing in her subjects, and that she wanted her father's approval (rather than "his penis"). Anyhow, I felt utterly devastated.

Yet while Joanne was at the hospital, my own life took an unexpected turn. We had an upstairs neighbor named Darla who was from Oklahoma, and who had a furry pet mink. She was heading back to live at home the very next day. But in the middle of the night, she knocked on my door. She stood there wearing a loosely fitting night gown. We made love for some time until she left for home in the morning. I am so grateful to Darla for allowing me to enjoy intimacy and to learn what healthy sex and physical love were about. With that newfound inner strength, I was soon able to leave Joanne, and after some months I found a healthy relationship that lasted three years.

I first met Tina-Belle—her actual name—in my sophomore year. She was from Austin, Texas, where her parents were professors. Tina was wholesome, entirely different from Joanne. I met her in Mathew Alpern's physiological vision lab, where I was working on an independent research project, and where Tina was employed as his secretary. This was the first time I experienced a melding of intense sexual attraction and romantic love. I courted Tina for some weeks and even had dinner with her parents a few times. They were now professors in the social work department at Michigan. At one of these enjoyable meals, I learned they were close friends with Pete Seeger, the iconic leftist folk singer, and that Tina had learned some songs from him, which she played for me on her guitar. I was in love. I probably over-romanticized our relationship, but it was wonderful, and it changed the direction of my life.

From Ann Arbor, Michigan, I was next off to Berkeley, California, for graduate school in medical biophysics. As one coming of age in the unrestrained 1960s with "sex, drugs, and rock and roll," casual sex was the norm. So I regressed and had lots of sex but very little in the way of warm, deep erotic connection. Thankfully, as I grew to understand my need for authentic relationships, I started dating Becky. With her, I learned I was with another feeling, sentient human being, not just an object to "screw."

As I consider the course of my life, I now count myself as being blessed with some of the most precious, deeply caring woman, who have accepted me even with some of my awkward struggles and have often facilitated my sexual and emotional growth with their open sensual kindness. What I learned, with each relationship, was to treasure Eros and make a connection to my spiritual being.

Eros in the Consulting Room

In reflecting on Eros, I considered many of its possible definitions and descriptions. These range from those of the ancient Greeks— the myth of Eros and Psyche—to definitions by various philosophers and, later, influential psychologists, particularly Freud, Jung, and Reich. It is my experience that Eros is equivalent to "life energy." Freud concurs on this point and would state that Eros is not to be confused with libido. It is not exclusively the sex drive, but, rather, is our life force and the will to live. Eros, more broadly, is simply the desire to create, or procreate, life. As such, it often manifests as creativity and productivity.

When I work with individuals, they often report bodily sensations of tingling, vibration, shaking, trembling, spontaneous full breath, and waves of warmth or coolness. I might ask them to follow those sensations and then to say a set of scripted words, while noticing what transpires within themselves. I may prefix this invitation by adding, "Of course, these are my words, but I invite you to notice what happens inside you when you say this sentence: 'I am alive, I'm alive; I'm alive and I'm real!'

One of two outcomes are common. First, the sensations may increase, in which case I generally encourage the individual to open to them. On the other hand, the sensations may be tamped down or cut off when they say those same words. In that case, I might have them explore the meaning of such a statement: what goes on inside their body and mind when they vocalize the words, and particularly what thoughts come up. Frequently the client perceives their own aliveness as dangerous because, during their childhood, one or both of their parents or guardians could not handle their natural exuberance. Likely this was when the parents were chronically overwhelmed, intoxicated, anxious, or depressed.

Perhaps you, dear reader, might experiment now with saying these words, and notice what happens as you make this affirming statement: "I am alive, I'm alive; I'm alive and I'm real!"

Let us also address how these words might impact someone, like myself and some of you, who has endured sexual abuse or assault. Unfortunately sexual abuse and rape are all too common. Statistically, likely between forty and fifty percent of people have lived through some sort of sexual trauma. When the above words are spoken by survivors, the simple act of saying them might trigger defense mechanisms of deflection and avoidance.

So then, what does it take to heal? My hope is that my story of healing might be useful for therapists, and to all who seek wellness. For me it was necessary to first address how my body recoiled from the violence of my past rape. This was probably the easier, or more obvious, part of my healing journey, because it related clearly to how my body contracted and dissociated from this core insult. The other, more hidden aspects of my sexual wounding were like the riptides in the ocean, hidden from view. These powerful undercurrents traced back to my mother's rejecting my innocent five-year-old sexuality. In addition, there was my father's squashing of my adolescent exploration with Barry. So while the rape was clear and concrete, these other influences were only slowly uncovered, in my case, through supportive, open, and caring erotic relationships.

These relationships involved attraction, playful flirting, sharing walks and meals, hand holding, and eventual lying together, clothes on, and following our breathing. Next, we would lie together naked without sexual intercourse. And always, through each of these steps, we would sense and share our body sensations, thoughts, and memories. If I or they felt somehow stuck, we would explore the nature of this stuck-ness, attending to the sensations, emotions, images, and thoughts.

"Eros" as used here is, at its root, "life energy." Libido is a natural force that brings us into intimate relationships. But Eros is much more than that. It is not exclusively the sex drive, but rather, how we fully live and embody our life force as expressed throughout our lives. Eros ultimately is the desire to create—or procreate—life, and to enhance our creativity. For me, even writing this book, difficult as it was, is an expression of Eros. To quote Wilhelm Reich, "Love, work and knowledge should be the wellspring of our life, they should also govern it." For me this is the essence of Eros. So then the question is, how do we use this spark to support deep healing and the embracing of a vibrant life?

September 1996:
The Green Sweater

Ring the bells that still can ring
Forget your perfect offering
There is a crack in everything
That's how the light gets in

LEONARD COHEN, "ANTHEM"

I've had the privilege to teach in Copenhagen, Denmark, at the Bodynamic Institute and then, for several years, with the OASIS Centre for Treatment and Rehabilitation of Victims of Torture and Trauma, which works with refugees and torture victims. In September of 1996, I was anxious about my upcoming trip to Europe. I am markedly uncomfortable with air travel and choose, whenever possible, to submit myself to the rude and unreliable rail service of Amtrak and spend days instead of hours traveling. (Though, of course, train travel in Europe is quite comfortable and reliable.) I have a congenital form of hemolytic anemia that makes sudden pressure changes unhealthy. In traveling to Europe, I was about to be placed into a high-altitude pressurized sardine can for fifteen hours.

Waiting nervously until the last possible minute to board, I was unexpectedly denied the right to bring my carry-on luggage. Chaotically, I repacked some items into a nylon bag so I could take my writing work and valuables with me on the plane. As the bulkhead doors closed, I reached to my shoulder where I thought my sweater was draped. Instead, I found nothing. My heart plummeted into the empty pit of my stomach—I felt sick. In the scurry over the carry on, the beautiful green sweater I had bought for this trip had disappeared.

Because of my economic situation at that time, I rarely bought new clothing; though thankfully, this tendency toward intense frugality has since greatly improved. I imagine this "poverty mentality" had much to do with the time our family was in dire financial straits due to my father's court battles and eventual imprisonment. In any case, I had fallen in love with this sturdy, warm piece of thick cotton weave. It truly made me feel cozy and glad. Shimmering with the deep green of a primeval forest, the sweater, like a security blanket, was to be my warm traveling companion in Europe.

I arrived a few minutes early in civilized Copenhagen and made it through their brief customs inspection. After a few perfunctory words exchanged in Danish, I was left with forty minutes before my host came to meet me. I rushed to the Scandinavian Airlines System (SAS) office and threw myself on their kind mercy. I implored them to find the phone number of the Seattle-Tacoma "Sea-Tac" International Airport lost and found. Each day I phoned both SAS and Sea-Tac. My initial optimism waned by the end of the week. Many calls and seventy-two hours later, I was faced both with jet lag and the reality of the loss of my beloved sweater.

My time teaching in Denmark passed quickly. Next on the itinerary was a short stay in Munich, Germany. There I happened to meet a lovely young physician. I had not been in a sexual relationship for a couple of years, and so I was excited as the flirtation developed. We made plans to rendezvous that weekend in Garmisch-Partenkirchen, where I was to address an International Congress on Humanistic Medicine. It was mid-October and the evenings were getting quite chilly at this high altitude. Again I felt pangs of loss for my green sweater. But it was time, I realized, to let go and move on.

Garmisch-Partenkirchen, Germany, and Aspen, Colorado, are "sister cities." In addition to their formidable mountain grandeur, both offer upscale, fashionable shops. In these shops there were precious few sweaters in the under–1,200 Deutsche Mark (DM) range, or about $1,400 USD at that time. It appeared there was no affordable replacement for my sweater to be found. I did, though, come across a slightly torn alpaca wool sweater from South America for 150 DM. This seemed like an affordable option; but no, I would wait. It just wasn't the right sweater. However, that evening, upon returning to my hotel, I saw a beautiful green, orange, blue, and brown sweater laid out artistically in the window display of a classy clothing store. The shop had just closed. The next morning, I rushed to the chic store, hoping no one got there before me. I gasped at the price of 600 DM, or about $750 USD. In a manner very uncharacteristic of a German shopkeeper, the stiffly dressed owner must have sensed both my excitement and my limited resources, and offered it to me at his cost, about 200 DM. Eagerly I put it on, paid him, and then joyfully walked back to my hotel. I had found precisely the right sweater!

I had a few moments before my lecture to call my date for the weekend. Her receptionist put me through. I told her I would be happy to see her that weekend, but she would need to have her own room. When she asked why, I said that I was sure it would have been exciting and fun, but it was not the right fit; it was not the right sweater! I would wait. She thanked me for my honesty. We never saw each other again.

That evening, while having dinner with my hosts at a restaurant called the Glass Pavilion, I glanced up to an adjacent table and saw a woman with a numinous presence, elegance, and rare splendor. She truly took my breath away. I stopped speaking with my colleagues and stared toward the table where she was sitting with three other people. I needed to approach her. I excused myself to go to the WC, or toilet, which was just past her table on the left. Her deep brown skin suggested she was perhaps Indonesian or Indian. Her black-opal eyes and dark hair were entirely of another world. As I passed by her table, my body turned, ever so slightly, toward her. Unable to find the right words, I took two awkward steps away and then disappeared into the men's room. I wondered if she had noticed me, and what she might have thought about my erratic approach. Inside the WC, I looked in the mirror and saw a face I did not recognize—at the same time, I seemed both younger and older.

That night I had a dream in which I asked God if I would ever be happy. A compassionate but firm voice answered, "No." Though God softly added that if I completed the task of getting my work into the world, particularly to the medical and scientific communities, my next lifetime would not be as painful and troubled as this one had been. *Some consolation*, I thought! Upon waking, I recalled my previous dream with the boat on the Hudson River and the blinking green light, in which I wasn't listening to God when She/He spoke to me. But this time She/He certainly had grabbed my attention! It appeared that my karma (destiny) and dharma (work) were to be one and the same, or at least inexorably wedded.

During the next couple days, I requested of my hosts that we dine again and again at the Glass Pavilion. My lame excuse was that I liked the food there; though it was in actuality rather ordinary. I saw this mystery woman twice. Both times, however, she was accompanied by the same man who had been sitting with her the first time. I was disheartened. Yet on Sunday afternoon, at the final session of the congress, I saw the mysterious woman walk into the conference hall, without the man who had seemed to be her companion. I followed her in but lost her in the main hall.

Suddenly my shoulder twisted to the right, and then, without question, the rest of my body followed. With a rush of fear combined with a sense of purpose and courage, I walked down the right aisle and found her sitting together with a woman friend. I turned toward her and said something like: "Excuse me, you have the most beautiful eyes I've ever seen—the most beautiful in the world, or perhaps in the universe! But I guess you already know that." She looked up at me, seemingly puzzled.

I stood there as though frozen by Medusa's gaze. She spoke a few words to me in German. Unable to speak again myself, I broke into a fiery-hot sweat. I forced a smile and then retreated to the lobby. I had to do something to busy myself so as not to feel my terror and aloneness. So I perused the book table. I had a whirl of confused thoughts, as if my mind were deflecting awareness from the depth of my encounter moments ago. Then, as I left the conference hall and stepped into the crisp mountain-night air, glad for the warmth of my beloved new sweater, a voice called out behind me. As I turned, I was jolted as by an electric shock. I stopped as the mystery woman approached me. She spoke at last: "You have come to me at the Glass Pavilion," she said—so apparently she did notice me there. "And then, just now, in the auditorium. So now I come to you. In Germany, we have an expression that good things happen in threes. My name is Sanju. I haven't spoken English for twelve years. If we get to know each other, I will sometime tell you why." While I don't actually recall the specifics, it had something about being beaten up by her family for marrying a non-Indian German man. Then out of nowhere she asked me, as in the dream, "Are you happy?" Stunned by her inquiry, I was literally speechless. After regaining my ground, I responded, "I am not happy." Though I added that I had just asked God this very same question. But how did she know? To say I was thrown off-center would have been a glaring understatement. Over the time we were together,

I was to be guided many times by this apparent sorceress, whose name, as it happened, meant "joy" in Hindi.

After some moments, I dared to asked Sanju if she would possibly meet me in Munich during the coming week. Astonishingly, she agreed and then traveled almost eight hours by train from Bochum to meet me at my hotel, which overlooked the lovely English Garden park in Munich. After teaching that day, I returned to the hotel and went to the front desk and asked if a young woman had come to see me. The man called up and, as per her instructions, gave me her room number. I walked up to the room, knocked on the door, and then entered into a space like a tantric temple, replete with many candles and soft fabrics draped over the lamps.

After this encounter, we carried on a long-distance relationship for three years, though it was only after two years that we finally made physical love. We were in Holland at that time and, as I slowly penetrated her sacred Yoni, I felt my body dissolve into nothingness, an infinite black void; as black as her eyes. As I later realized, this was something akin to an "ego death." It was indeed my first encounter with the Vajrayogini, the "trauma goddess" in Tibetan Buddhism. As I understand, this archetype represents the great wisdom that emerges in transforming a trauma. I have a Tibetan friend who confirmed this and gave me a beautiful thangka where this goddess was crushing a skull with her feet (representing the destruction of the false ego). With Sanju, my "persona" was disintegrating. A part of my personality was utterly shattered, and a new part was not yet born.

During these times, my grief grew so intense it threatened to annihilate me. For seemingly no reason, I would sob in wrenching convulsions, a pain deeper than I could ever remember feeling. When our physical relationship finally ended three years later, I felt only appreciation and gratitude.

July 1998: Lyons, Colorado

When Lucy first met my mother at Hunter College, the year they were both freshmen, she fell completely and utterly in love with her. She would sit and wait on a bench for long stretches of time just to get a glimpse of my mother, Helen. Lucy would even sacrifice some of her classes to have the opportunity to talk with her. See plate 5 for a photo of my mother in her youth.

In the sixty years since their college days, Lucy, her husband Al, and my mother had remained the closest of friends, even as Lucy and Al moved west from New York to Colorado. In a seeming coincidence, they would live a few miles from my Apple Valley house in Lyons, Colorado, located in the foothills of the Rocky Mountains. My mother and Leonard, her romantic partner of fifteen years, called to let me know they would be coming out to see Lucy and Al the following week. It was Al's ninety-fifth birthday, and he and Lucy would be moving from their mountain home in Lyons to the town of Boulder before the winter snow. Helen and Leonard had shared much bird-watching time together with Al and Lucy in the latter couple's avian paradise where the only sounds to be heard were the songs of the many species of birds that made their homes among the large, open meadows and surrounding rock cliffs. Sanju was also flying in from Germany at the end of that same week.

When she arrived, Sanju and I joined Helen, Leonard, Lucy, and the nonagenarian Al for lunch. The moment we got there, my mother abruptly rose from the table and embraced Sanju, hugging her tightly as though she were a long-lost daughter. This overt show of affection had never happened with any of my previous girlfriends; with them, she seemed indifferent, even cold and remote.

I was about to have my fifty-six-year-old shell cracked open. I did not expect a frontal attack upon my relationship with my mother and the roots of my emotional armoring. Sanju would soon expose a primordial crack in the paleontological strata of my psyche and release a deeply buried genie that would open my heart. It was an erotic awakening that would shatter my protective shell and take me over the edge of a precipice I had resisted for a lifetime. I was ready to let the light shine through this crack in the cosmic egg.

When Helen and Lucy first met at Hunter College, nothing could keep them apart, not even my eventual father. Morris met the college "twin sisters" during one of their animated scientific, artistic, and philosophic discussions. Attracted to both beauties, he was only allowed to hang out at the periphery of their all-consuming relationship. When Sanju heard this story during our lunch gathering, she asked my mother and Lucy if they'd had boyfriends. "Well, yes," Lucy said, "we did have a few boyfriends. But we discouraged most men who approached us." I imagined this was because of the intensity and breadth of their sisterly relationship. Then, to everyone's surprise, Sanju asked Lucy if she'd had sex with her boyfriend. The ever-ready, ever-witty octogenarian did not lose a beat in replying: "Well, dear, in those days we weren't supposed to, but of course some of us did!"

Almost coughing my tea back into the cup, I gasped as Sanju now turned her attention toward my mother. Feigning innocence, Sanju asked my mother, "Who was your boyfriend, Helen?"

Lucy offered, "He was a man named Albert" (pronounced Ahlbeer).

In the seconds of silence that followed, my mother looked shyly down at the table. I held my breath with unease. What would my mother say if Sanju asked her the same sexual question she had asked

Lucy? Instead, Sanju inquired, "Were you in love with him, Helen?" My mother fumbled and answered that they were just dating.

Yet before Sanju could say anything more, Lucy looked directly across the table at her lifelong friend and said, "Yes, Helen you were. You were deeply in love with him."

I saw the tender look in Lucy's eyes as she gazed firmly but gently into my mother's. I visualized the pure love between the two adolescent girls sitting across from each other on the bench sixty-plus years before. There was a softness in my mother's face, something I had rarely seen. I sensed my mother's deep internal conflict over whether to regain her defensive rigidity, or allow this deep emotional truth to surface.

As she struggled, I also floundered in my attempt to engage with the mother I would have never known, but for Sanju's provocative mischief. "Mother," I said, "tell me about this man, please."

"His name was Albert Mangonès," she said. "He was studying architecture. He was also a poet and artist; and he taught me some folk songs from Haiti." My mother began to sing, choosing the courageous path of the heart. Albert's father, she added, was the mayor of Port-au-Prince. According to my mother, he was also the leader of the opposition party against the ruthless Haitian dictator, François "Papa Doc" Duvalier.

I quietly sobbed inside. I grasped now, for the first time, the source of a deep wound to my psyche, body, and soul. A "cellular mystery" had been raised and comprehended. At the age of fifty-six I was given the clue, the missing piece of the puzzle, that would lead to an awakening. I understood for the first time why, in spite of her enduring support in many ways, I was still my mother's hated child. I saw in a blinding insight—or "inside"— why she despised my father and why she believed I was a product of his raping her. It all made sense: I was not the offspring of her first and truest love, Albert Mangonès. My mother's parents, I reasoned, must have pressured her to marry my father, Morris. After all he was Jewish, bright, handsome, charming, and white! My mother's daring to date a Black man at the time of the outbreak of the Second World War filled me both with pride and admiration. That she was deeply in love with him, that they really had read poetry and sung together, awakened a heart opening and a long-suppressed sexual yearning in me. I now, strangely, had two fathers, one white and the other Black. There was no need to forgive my mother; I understood, in my body, the truth of love, and thus I could let go and move forward. The seventeenth-century polymath Blaise Pascal wrote, poignantly, that "the heart has its reasons which reason does not know."

Having let down her walls at last, my mother told more of the story: "Peter, when you were three years old, Albert came to visit me." It was his only visit. I imagined they were both still in love with each other. How painful this bittersweet meeting must have been for them. While Albert was at our apartment, my mother explained, I was constructing a house out of blocks of wood. "Your father and I were utterly astonished at the complexity of the design and your ability to balance these large pieces of wood into a make-believe house," my mother said. "Albert sat by your side and was even more amazed at your architectural intuition." I wondered where this interest in architecture might have come from. Was it possibly somehow transmitted from Albert, my mother's true love, this new spiritual "second father" of mine? She continued, "You were doing things with wooden blocks that most kids don't do until they're seven or eight." But one of my constructions collapsed, and I broke down crying. Then, my mother said, "Albert patiently showed you how to make a cantilevered beam to support the unbalanced weight of the house."

At that moment I felt myself surrounded by Helen's and Albert's love. My story was unfolding anew, previously missing parts fitting together. I was overcome with a deepening sense of peace and excitement at my new family: Morris, Albert, and even Leonard, my mother's new beau after my father's death.

At home that night, I sat with Sanju. I needed to sort through the impact of my mother's revelations. While we were sitting quietly together, I began to softly tremble. I don't know how to describe an injury so profound that it penetrates the soul and undermines the progress of one's life direction. I think of a sapling that has been twisted during planting, and how its expression at maturity is gnarled and tangled. Or a crack as deep as the Grand Canyon that collects and diverts the rain and the rivers from the vast lands within and beyond its reach. I now felt that my wounding was less a personal injury and more akin to these universal forces of nature. Yes, I had been deeply and primally wounded as a child—and had, at different stages of my life, felt the scars of this deep wounding. I was now surrendering to a free fall so deep that I again feared annihilation. I had always felt I was a product of hate. Instead, I was now being held and healed by ancestral love.

Some years before my mother recounted her love story, I had unexpectedly remembered being raped by the mafia thugs when I was a preteen. As previously stated, I told my mother about this. I remember she froze as the color drained from her face. I was afraid I had said too much. Her color gradually returned, and she spoke quickly, as though trying to get her thoughts out before she could close them off again: "Peter, I don't believe that rape really happened. Instead, your father raped me—that's how you were conceived."

Both were true. Yes I was really raped, and yes I was exposed in utero to my mother's experience of being raped by my father. She felt raped, but really, I conjectured, her hatred of my father (and of me in turn) came out of the heartbreak of losing her first love, Albert. I wondered if she ever got over this loss. Somehow I was less startled by the knowledge of this part of her life than I was by her willingness to reveal to me a story that must have weighed so heavily on her heart—to the point that when my father was struggling with the mafia testimony, she had a "nervous breakdown" out of fear and guilt.

With my new knowledge of my mother's past, I was able to put some distance between myself and the undercurrent of guilt, shame, and self-hatred I had always felt. It became apparent that my having been conceived in hatred was why I was poorly nurtured as an infant and why my mother and I never really bonded and securely attached. This had been problematic for me with various lovers over the years.

What happened at that lunch table gifted me a bigger picture. Of course, she hated me. How could it be otherwise, and how could I not hate myself? She could not marry the man she loved, and she felt raped by the man she blamed for her loss, my father. I felt a deep compassion both for her loss and for my lifelong pain. Sanju held me; I grieved for all of us.

Sanju reminded me of how Albert and I had sat together at age three with my building blocks, he at my side, admiring my creative work. Could I picture him? I had no clear memory of him, but I let my imagination journey back to my encounter with Albert. I was now a three-year-old child sitting by the side of this beautiful, strong, yet tender Black man, so different from my conception of maleness until then. He was attentive and playful, and he guided without intrusion, without diminishing my own power and creative process. He watched me make mistakes and, with his gentle advice, I learned from them. He never judged my missteps and smiled warmly as I gained a new understanding of the relationship of the laws of architecture with those of gravity. *Boom*: the dozen blocks I'd worked so hard to balance in my emerging structure crashed to the ground. I began to cry. He gently held my hand and assisted me in finding a better balance the next time. But they were always my ideas; he only prompted. I laughed, throwing my arms up in joy. My internal support was solidifying in the presence of this sweet, kind man from Haiti.

My history of romantic relationships has sometimes been a tortured one—both for my mates and myself. These relationships have, at times, been fraught with disappointment and misunderstanding. I've been afraid of powerful women, and at the base of it, terrified of my own power and sexuality. But now, in part because of gaining conscious awareness of my encounter with Albert, I have since felt seen, nourished, and challenged by a number of powerful and wonderful women who, thankfully, have come into my life. And with Sanju, I was able to uncouple my own surrender to orgasm from the rape by the mafia and the rape by which I was conceived.

Through this loving, creative awakening that I was enjoying with Albert, I was able to rewrite the story of my childhood. Side by side with this poetic, vibrant, erotically alive, and quietly powerful man, a dormant snake coiled deeply in the root of my spine rose up: my emergent sexuality and lust for life.

My new family grew; first it had two members, Albert and Leonard, my mother's live-in boyfriend; and then it expanded to include Albert, Leonard, my mother Helen, and Morris, my biological father. The wounds of betrayal were lifted. There was instead a shared affection between Morris and Leonard. They both loved the same woman. As we all gathered together, Leonard and Albert sat closest to Helen while Morris sat a little further away. I was now in a field of shifting relationships and sensual awakenings. A field of new possibilities for my future love relationships. I was gradually learning to love and be loved, to hold and to be held, thanks to my new family.

Summer 1998: Aspen, Colorado

The next day, after our lunch with Lucy and my mother, Sanju and I left for three weeks together in Aspen, carrying with us the internalized images of Albert Mangonès, Helen, Morris, and Leonard. A friend had arranged for us to caretake an old homestead ranch on Red Mountain overlooking the city of Aspen and the majestic Maroon Bells. I was to continue a painful and sometimes joyous journey of awakening over the next month. This waking would catalyze a rebirth, the beginning of an autonomous, erotic, loving self. During this time, Sanju and I also had our share of arguments and misunderstandings. Most were challenges relating to different schools of thought on relationships. Our shadows rose to the challenge of owning our myriad projections and learning to be with ourselves and with each other in a more authentic way. At the end of our stay in Aspen, I had the following dream: Sanju and I were sitting back-to-back and looking out in opposite directions. I awoke with tears of gratitude for our meetings together and knew that we would now be parting ways, each going in our own direction.

I now consider the meaning of my green sweater, which is more than a symbol: it is, rather, an embodied metaphor for Life, Love, and Choice. According to the dictionary, *metaphor* comes from a Latin word meaning "to carry over," or a vessel or container to carry forward or bring forth. In this sense, my green sweater was an object that I loved and lost. It became an idealized form that I projected out and measured all other sweaters by, in vain. I had to let it go in order to realize my delight in a new sweater, and in the right relationship.

As I reflect on my relationships with the women I've known over the past decades, I believe that much confusion, ambiguity, and pain was created because of my disconnect from the universal, embracing Great Goddess and my projection of that archetype onto these lovers. At the same time, I have an immense gratitude for several of these women's support as they allowed me to project that goddess archetype onto them. In this way I was able to gradually absorb some of my projections, and to connect with their deep feminine energies within myself. Both through brief romantic encounters and long-term relationships, I began to open to my "anima," the term used by Jung to describe the feminine living within the man.

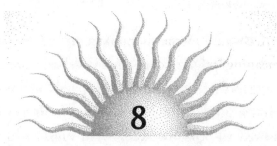

Many Cultures, One Race: The Human Race

I have always been fascinated by the diversity of cultures and traditions on this good earth. So it is gratifying that my life has given me the opportunity to visit and explore some unique settings in how different cultures heal trauma. Peoples of different eras and different regions have, in their own ways, dealt with loss, pain, helplessness, and despair. It is with humility and gratitude that I acknowledge how much I have gained from these rich opportunities. What follows is an exploration of some of these encounters, which have influenced my path and my being.

Henrique

During my nomadic wanderings, one of my most precious and unique connections was with Henrique Perret Neto. I suppose he could be considered a shaman, although in Brazil someone with these gifts might rather be called a "Pai de Santo," or "Father Saint," in Brazilian Portuguese. This is a syncretic spiritual tradition, one that blends aspects of other ones. For Henrique it was the African deities (the Orixás), indigenous shamanic influences, Western Spiritism, and elements of Christianity.

In November 2004, my mother died. I had met Henrique Neto some years before and, prior to her untimely death, had already arranged to meet with him again in early March of 2005. At the time, few people knew of my mother's passing besides myself, my brothers, and her partner Leonard, who explained to us that she had drowned in the bathtub. I had been trying for five years to get the two of them to relocate from New York City to Berkeley, California, due to my mother's declining health and chronic pain. The move would have allowed them to be near my brothers: Bob, who practiced acupuncture; and Jon, one of the world's foremost authorities on pain.

Besides feeling shock and grief, I fretted over the possibility she had committed suicide. Though, much later, I learned she had died of an accidental overdose of opioid painkillers. My mother had vehemently resisted my urging her to give up the New York apartment, where she had lived since her childhood. Furthermore, I thought she felt significant remorse and guilt about the ways she had psychologically injured me, from birth onward.

I decided to follow through with my plans to visit Henrique. So, in March 2005, my partner Laura and I traveled to Ouro Prêto, literally "Black Gold," in the Brazilian countryside a couple hours north of Belo Horizonte. Early the next morning, we were brought to Henrique's healing center deep in a jungle clearing. As we exited the car, we were greeted by Henrique and several rotund, spiritually grounded Bahia women from the state of Bahia in Northeast Brazil, who wore long white dresses. As they encircled us, they graciously welcomed us with flowers and song.

Chanting and swaying, they transported us into a quiet and subtle trance. To complete our introduction, Henrique engaged a special ritual. He placed a glass full of water on top of each of our heads. It was only after we were able to remain perfectly, internally still, such that the glass of water rested securely atop our heads, that Henrique invited us into their simple house of worship.

As we walked slowly around the *fazenda* (farm), Henrique picked some seemingly unremarkable flowers, herbs, and *folhas* (leaves). He dropped them casually onto a table and then guided us to an outdoor eating area where we shared a wonderful lunch, prepared and offered by the Bahia women. After this delicious but simple feast, we came back to the table and, amazingly, the leaves and flowers had opened into a perfectly symmetrical and exquisitely beautiful mandala—an arrangement not unlike the intricate and utterly transient Tibetan sand paintings. It was truly phenomenal. Henrique then made a circle out of concentric necklaces and emptied many small shells from a special beaded pouch into the center. These sacred divination shells are called *búzios*—Portuguese for "shells." Henrique would turn them over in his cupped hands and, after a moment of meditation, toss them into the middle of the necklace ring. See plate 6. He did this several times, and each time, he went into a trance of deep reflection. Finally he looked up at me with a warm yet neutral gaze. He said, "Peter, your mother died recently, and it wasn't suicide." With those few kind words, a wave of relief rolled through me. He went on to say, "Your mother apologizes for what she did to you and wants to let you know she loves you; and if you wish, she can support you from the other side." Tears of relief and gratitude filled my eyes. It seemed as if we accomplished a decade's worth of therapy in that short reading of the *búzios*.

The Krenek

On a different visit to Brazil, with the help of a student and colleague named Ana do Valle, I had the opportunity to visit the Krenek peoples. This is a remote tribe, one that took us thirty hours of travel to reach before we finally met the chief and his daughter, the princess. Because our travel plans had unraveled, we missed trekking in the early morning, so we arrived in sweltering, near-hundred-degree sun. So with a previously frozen, now semi-poached fish in hand, we made a traditional gift offering.

The chief took one look at me and ushered me to a hole in some rocks, which spouted a light shower of cool water. He then motioned me to come behind their simple house to sit together on bamboo mats under a mango tree. Next, he offered me one of the wooden flutes he'd brought with him. We played together for twenty timeless minutes. He seemed to notice that something had settled within me, and only then did he ask why I had come.

I inquired if he knew of the term "Sustos"—Portuguese for "fright paralysis." He said yes and added that his daughter had also told him about the word "trauma." In his understanding, trauma didn't exist in isolation. It was not something that happened to the individual, but rather only occurred when there was a break in the connection between members of a tribe—or in our terms, a society. Thus, since trauma occurred in the group, it had to be healed in the group. This wisdom has stayed with me, and is now recognized by some current traumatologists, who have come to a similar understanding. In our modern isolated societies we have gained technological advances; however, we have lost the salubrious climate of belonging, of support from others in our community.

Later in the day, I asked the chief if I could ride the horse that was tied to a tree close by. He said yes and I headed up a hill. Unbeknownst to me, I was riding the princess's horse—everyone had a good laugh about that when I returned. Then our talk became more serious. First the chief asked me where I had gone on the ride. I described my journey: up the hill and then navigating a sharp left turn into a clearing. The people gathered, looked at me intently, and then informed me I had gone to a sacred place where the ancestors were buried. After this they opened to me, and we discussed many topics. The chief told me how they worked with dreams. Generally, when a person had a disturbing or illuminating dream, the entire group would come together and perform a ceremony, sharing the dream and acting it out through chanting and dancing.

I also learned that several weeks prior to our arrival, one of the young women, who had diabetes, was pregnant with twins. Because of her high risk, she was taken to the only hospital a few hours away. Tragically both twins died and needed to be extricated by caesarian section. The woman fell into a severe depression and the hospital was planning to administer shock treatment. So in the middle of the night, some of the tribe members fashioned a ladder to reach her window, thus rescuing her from that brutal treatment.

Every night, the tribe assembled to do their ritual dance movements, and they invited us to join. The young woman who had endured the horrific ordeal at the hospital sat on the periphery of the circle. Nothing was expected of her; she was included only as much as she wished. Then, after some nights, she came to join the circle. It seemed as though everyone started to cry, and the young woman broke down in wrenching tears of grief. Her depression lifted, and thereafter she joined in the ritual dance. When we participated, performing the simple steps in unison, we entered an altered state of consciousness, a state that clearly helped create a cohesion among the entire tribe. This is something we are sorely missing in our secularized, fragmented, and individualistic societies. The lack of such deep connection is a great detriment to our individual and collective well-being.

Hopi

I also received some momentous spiritual blessings when I lived in Flagstaff, Arizona in the 1980s and taught at the Hopi Guidance Center in the village of Shungopavi, located on the Second Mesa. The village had a breathtaking view of the San Franciscan peaks, the home and resting place of the kachinas (the Hopi sacred deities). When teaching at the Guidance Center, I once again acquired a deepened appreciation for the need to address the collective, and not just the individual, in healing the wounds of trauma.

Usually when I teach, I demonstrate with one of the students, and then they practice with each other. When teaching at the Guidance Center, I asked for a volunteer; however, no one would offer themselves, even with my gentle coaxing. I assumed this reticence was due to the understanding that you don't expose your family's secrets. Or perhaps these students simply felt shy around an outsider.

When having lunch with an anthropologist, I spoke to him about my difficulties. What surfaced from our discussion was that, in Hopi culture, there is no such thing as an individual, not as we in the West know it. They see the basic units of society as the family, village, and tribe. When he conveyed this difference to me, I realized I had gone about my invitation the wrong way. At my next meeting with my Hopi students, I asked one of the highly trained and sophisticated therapists at the center to present one of their cases. There was immediate and enthusiastic engagement. After the presentation, I asked if any of the members of the training class had had a similar experience to the presented client. To that query, a student immediately volunteered for an in-class demonstration. This was held as an opportunity for the group member, the volunteer, to aid the therapist's outside client. To have the chance to contribute to the benefit of another was the powerful motivating force.

In many ways I learned more from the Hopi than they learned from me. To be embraced by their spiritual community was in itself a great privilege. However, it was the robust understanding of community-based healing that emerged, again, as a striking revelation. This invaluable insight, revealed amidst the tight-knit communities of the Brazilian Krenek tribe, underscored the essential role of communal cohesion in fostering wellness.

The Hopi offered me another gift when they invited me to observe some of their sacred dances. One of these dances was a vitally important and traditional ritual called the rattlesnake dance. During this event, some members of the tribe danced with snakes hanging from their mouths. Once again, this was not a show of individual bravado, but rather a ceremonial communion, a deeply religious group invocation. It involved an elaborate series of prayers offered to their gods, principally to the Plumed Serpent. Through the rattlesnake dance, they asked for life-giving rain to save their corn, beans, and squash, as well as other crops that provide sustenance and life.

Navajo, the People, the Dine

My next-door neighbors in Flagstaff were a group of Navajo men. They were very appreciative of my spirit dog, Pouncer. His outgoing and friendly personality served as a bridge between our yards, our homes, and our cultures. After one of our conversations about my healing methods, they recognized my sincerity and invited me to meet with a medicine man whom they knew. After we met on several occasions, the medicine man invited me to a traditional ceremony, "The Enemy Way." This was used to reintegrate returning warriors back into the tribe. The Navajo understood that, without addressing their war traumas, the family, village, and ultimately the tribe would bear the brunt of the unhealed wounds. After this ritual, the warriors or veterans would continue to be honored and revered for their service, their sacrifice, by ritually opening powwows and taking the lead in parades. While this was the era of the Vietnam War, this tradition harkened back to when there were tribal wars, as well as times when many First Nation warriors were returning soldiers from other conflicts, including the so-called Indian Wars, the First and Second World Wars, and the Korean War.

During the Second World War, the Navajo as well as some other tribes had a language that was used to secretly communicate between different U.S. brigades. Because it was an unwritten language, they were able to translate and speak the commands to other troops that also had a Navajo man. These "Code Talkers" were in jeopardy of being killed, not only by the enemy, but by their own colleagues as well in order to prevent them from being captured and revealing their language code under torture. Because of the danger of being captured, they were given cyanide pills to carry with them, and their fellow troops were instructed to shoot the Code Talkers if there was any danger of their being caught. So you can imagine the threat they lived under and the courage it took to persevere. These were the extraordinary traumas they were bringing back to their villages and would need help cleansing and healing.

Let me briefly describe how the ritual reintegration was conducted. Before the warrior could return to his family, people would gather in a hogan—translated as "home"—a traditional round, domed dwelling of the Navajo people. Male tribe members formed a ring around a central fire. Drummers beat a rhythmic cadence, while the returning soldier circled the fire in step with the drumming. Meanwhile, a medicine man carefully watched the warrior who was moving around the fire, and counted backward through the years of the warrior's life. Each time the medicine man observed signs of trauma in the warrior's body, he noted the specific age at which a trauma had arisen, and his chants became more sonorous. The drumming intensified. The soldier's breath accelerated and his body movements changed, allowing for the release of his age-specific trauma within the healing circle of community. His deliverance was propelled by the crescendo of drumbeats, prayers, and chanting. These releases went on throughout the night until dawn arose. At this point the soldier faced the rising sun through the east door of the hogan. As he stepped into the light of dawn, he wretched and dispelled the "toxins" of the now-cleared trauma from the war, and also earlier or even childhood traumas. The returning warrior did not need to ruminate about his trauma history, since it was all in his body language as tracked by the medicine man.

Only after this release was the warrior reunited with his family and community at large. He was returned to a "state of balance and beauty within the universe," known as "Hózhó" in the Navajo language. How extraordinary it was to be included in this restorative healing ceremony!

The Enemy Way Ceremony, sometimes called the Squaw Dance, was used by the Navajo after World War II to "purify" and reintegrate the Code Talkers, who had faced such extreme peril during the war. See plate 7 for the watercolor, *First Furlough*, painted by Navajo artist Quincy Tahoma. Here is a prayerful song that was offered to them at the conclusion of the ceremony:

> Happily, may their roads back home be on the trail of pollen.
> Happily may they all get back.
> In beauty I walk.
> With beauty before me, I walk.
> With beauty behind me, I walk.
> With beauty below me, I walk.
> With beauty above me, I walk.
> With beauty all around me, I walk.
> It is finished in beauty,
> It is finished in beauty,
> It is finished in beauty,
> It is finished in beauty.[1]

While a soldier might receive multiple purification ceremonies, the deep respect and honor accorded to them by their communities also extend their healing throughout their remaining years. As a Ho-Chunk elder once said, "We honor our veterans for their bravery and because, by seeing death on the battlefield, they truly know the greatness of life."[2]*

---

*I have often noticed this layering of traumas with my clients when addressing a specific trauma. There might be other, earlier wounds that correspond to the later psychological injury. I have always been curious as to how these patterns of repetition might be like fractals embedded within other fractals.

Let There Be Light

In 1946 at the Mason Hospital on Long Island, New York, the U.S. Army created a healing environment for some of the World War II returning soldiers with PTSD, or "psychoneurosis" as it was then pejoratively known. In a sense this mirrored what happened with the Navajo rituals. But rather than using chanting, drumming, and prayer to induce trance, the hospital's "medicine men"—the esteemed physicians—used a powerful "truth serum," Sodium Pentothal. This created an intense altered state called hypno-narcosis. The doctors used this state to assist the soldiers in reviewing their traumas and divulging their terror, hopelessness, isolation, sense of impending doom, and the horrors of injury and mutilation. At the same time, shared housing, meals, and recreation—including baseball!—continued the bonding and togetherness that had previously characterized their military community. It was only after a month of this enclosed communal living that the families of the soldiers were allowed to rejoin their sons, husbands, and fathers.

This powerful experiment was filmed by the famous director John Huston. The military commissioned him to make this film to show that these returning "shell-shocked" troops could be reintegrated back into their pre-war lives as contributing members of society. What the army didn't expect was the revelation of how severely injured the veterans showed themselves to be. They feared the movie would be deeply disturbing to the populace at large and would be a deterrent to postwar recruitment. The film was subsequently banned, and so viewing was suppressed until 1980 when it was finally released. However, the copy that was eventually made public turned out to be of such poor quality that many of the conversations were inaudible. It remained available in this condition until 2010, when the National Film Preservation Foundation funded a refurbishing of the film. It can be viewed on YouTube, and I strongly recommend taking the time to watch it, so as to witness the healing and community spirit that were portrayed so poignantly.

John Huston claimed the military had banned his film "to maintain a 'warrior' myth, which said that our American soldiers went to war and came back all the stronger for the experience. . . . Everyone was a hero. . . . They might die, or they might be wounded, but their spirit remained unbroken."[3] While World War II veterans were considered the Greatest Generation's heroes, most did not get the type of healing support depicted in the film, but were still expected to return to their pre-war lives. All that the army leaders saw in the film was the soldiers' unacceptable weakness. They failed to understand that these men could heal gradually and become functioning and honored members of society; instead, their wounds were stigmatized and feared. Unlike the Navajo First Nation's deep appreciation and lifelong honoring of their warriors, we chose as a society to hide from this wounding and ignore the possible need for ongoing "purification," or therapeutic attention, and genuine respect.

American society's efforts toward soldiers' reintegration generally did not involve overt acknowledgment of their wounding and sacrifices, but instead created programs like the GI bill to address veterans' financial needs. This allowed them to buy houses in the suburbs, where they had material comfort but were deprived of the social cohesion of the Navajo hogans, villages, and tribes. They were provided with the means to go to college so they could become contributing members of society, but at the same time, they were forced to bury their traumas. The army and our society were unable to behold simultaneously that soldiers could have stark wounds of war and yet could slowly heal, perhaps then becoming even stronger, better leaders.

The Middle East: A Land of Endless Wars and Recycled Trauma

I was asked to teach a training in Jerusalem around 2002. I agreed to do the training only if Palestinian therapists were also invited to attend. This was no small task, but after some back-channel communication, several therapists from Gaza and the West Bank were able to participate. As you might imagine, this meeting was rather tense at first.

During a question and answer period, one participant asked me if it was possible to heal from a trauma if you didn't know where it originated. My short answer was yes. You need only recognize a troubling symptom, or some kind of "haunting." One Israeli then raised his hand to volunteer. His name was Chaim Dassberg, and he had pioneered psychoanalytic treatment for Holocaust survivors. Though he has long since passed away, during his lifetime I obtained his permission to use his full name.

Chaim reported he had been suffering from terrible lower back pain for thirty years. It was revealing to me that he attached this symptom to a precise time of origin, though he had no memory of this. I asked him to describe the pain, including its location, shape, and color. Next I guided him in exploring whether there was a particular tension that might underlie the pain. I followed this awareness by directing him to notice if the tension was equal on both sides—it wasn't. I then advised him to "imagine" what movement his body might want to make and then to follow that inner movement. At this point his breathing became rapid, and sweat dripped down his forehead. Clearly something deep was happening. He then reported having a memory that had been deeply repressed: During his time as an army doctor, his convoy was ambushed, and all the men except him were brutally murdered. Chaim survived only because he fell backward off the truck and rolled into a ditch. He landed on his back and remained still until the enemy soldiers had departed. Not only was he left with enduring back pain, but also a powerful dose of survivor's guilt.

Back to the class: At the end, I asked if anyone wanted to share their thoughts from observing the session. After some time, a psychologist from Gaza Mental Health Services stood up. She was tall and elegant and wore a gray business suit. She announced that when Chaim had volunteered for the session, she had hoped that something bad would happen to him, that he would be re-traumatized. She wanted him to know what he (or rather, the Israelis) had done to her people, how they had humiliated, tortured, and murdered them. But she continued: "Chaim, when I opened to your work with Dr. Levine, something happened inside me that I couldn't really understand. Without knowing why, I found myself praying for your healing. And, Chaim, I realized that until we find peace within ourselves, we will never find peace with each other." Sadly this peace has been elusive, as attacks and counterattacks continue to this day.

Germany

The past is never dead. It's not even past.

WILLIAM FAULKNER, *REQUIEM FOR A NUN*

When I first began teaching in Germany in 1982, I was overcome by episodes of anxiety, fear, and even bursts of panic. I attributed this anxiety simply to stage fright, perhaps due to the fear of working, for the first time, in this foreign country and this foreign language. Yet the fear seemed truly excessive.

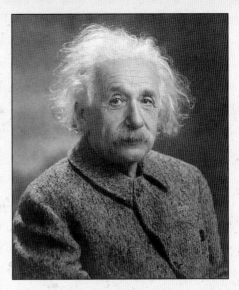

Plate 1. Johnny "Dio" Dioguardi, the Mafia captain who caused so much life-threat pain, not only for my family but a great many others during his life of crime and murder. He is an embodiment of the sort of intense trauma that the tiger within must be awakened to fight and overcome. *Credit: Bettmann.*

Plate 2. The disheveled professor with whom I enjoyed many helpful and healing conversations through active imagination. Albert Einstein would become, in a sense, my spirit guide. *Photograph by Oren Jack Turner, Princeton, N.J.*

Plate 3. Guarding stone at the entrance of the Celtic temple of Newgrange. This photograph immediately conveyed the meaning of my dream and made clear the task before me: to keep ancient wisdom alive. Indeed, dreams show the way. *Credit: Dave Keeshan, CC BY-SA 2.0.*

Plate 4. My father, Morris, in his late twenties. The memories that I have of my father singing songs and reading bedtime stories to me are some of my dearest.

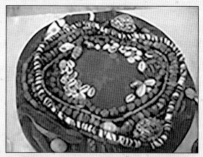

Plate 5. My mother, Helen, had dark, penetrating almond eyes and a bright intelligent mind. She was also gifted with remarkable faculties of intuition. I remain ever grateful for her support in my journey toward becoming a healer and teacher.

Plate 6. The instruments of cowrie shell divination or, as it is called in Brazil, *jogo de búzios*. With a reading of the *búzios*, my shamanic friend, Henrique, gave me much needed solace after my mother's death, which I mistakenly suspected may have been a suicide.

Plate 7. *First Furlough*, watercolor by Quincy Tahoma, Navajo artist. This lovely painting expresses the happiness that came back home along with the Navajo warriors who were supported to return to their families after their healing rituals. *Courtesy of the National Museum of the American Indian, Smithsonian Institution.*

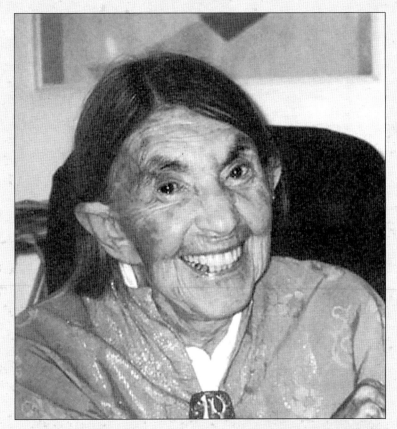

Plate 8. Charlotte Selver. One of my Sensory Awareness meditation teachers who taught me how to fully experience embodiment and connection with the world. A wonderful and vibrant woman who lived, loved, and taught until the age of 102. *Courtesy of Stefan Laeng.*

Plate 9. Charlotte alongside former Sensory Awareness student and colleague Judyth O. Weaver, who is also trained in SE. *Courtesy of Judyth O. Weaver.*

Plate 10. The indomitable Ida Rolf, who was also born in the Bronx and holds a special place in my heart as simply "Grandma." She taught me the importance of actually *seeing* what I'm looking at, a task that is not always so simple. Here she sits with a pink flower in her hair. *Courtesy of the Dr. Ida Rolf Institute®.*

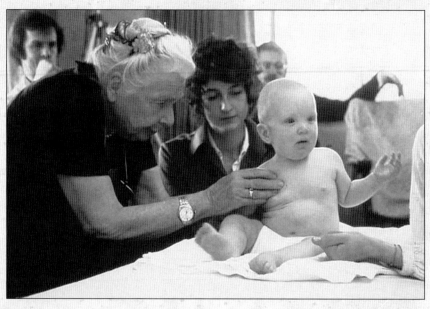

Plate 11. Ida working with a young client. Her insights into the importance of working with infants and children influenced my work considerably. *Courtesy of the Dr. Ida Rolf Institute®.*

Plate 12. Mira Rothenberg, author of *Children with Emerald Eyes* and one of my dearest mentors. Her work with emotionally disturbed and autistic children was awe inspiring. Blunt at times, tough, yet deeply compassionate, Mira was gifted with the rare ability to connect with even the most troubled youngsters. *Courtesy of Akiva Goldsman.*

Plate 13. Mira with her son, Akiva, sitting on the stoop of their Brooklyn brownstone. Kivie, as Mira called him, grew up to write the screenplay for the Academy Award–winning film *A Beautiful Mind,* among other well-known projects. *Courtesy of Akiva Goldsman.*

Plate 14. Aharon Katchalsky, acclaimed scientist and one of my postgraduate biophysics professors. His brilliant mathematical mind, while at times beyond me, ultimately inspired my work. Sadly, his life was taken in a 1974 terrorist attack at Ben Gurion Airport. *Courtesy of the Weizmann Institute.*

Plate 15. Ilya Prigogine, winner of the 1977 Nobel Prize in Chemistry. His work on dissipative structures and conclusions of "negative entropy" opened a portal into my understanding of titration: slowly and gently introducing only the right amount of trauma stimuli to regulate the nervous system. With proper dosage, the poison is the cure. *Public domain.*

Plate 16. René Thom, inventor of catastrophe theory and dreamer among intellectuals. His calculations articulate how slow changes in nature can yield sudden and drastic results. Applying his ideas to the nervous system also supported my use of titration. *Source: Konrad Jacobs, Erlangen, © MFO, CC BY-SA 2.0.*

Plate 17 and Plate 18. Consider these two images and pay attention to what you feel in your body. What thoughts do these images produce in your mind? If you were a newborn, which would you choose? *Plate 17: Image provided courtesy of Dotdash Meredith, Ladies' Home Journal®, 1945.*

Plate 19. Euphrasia Nyaki or, as I know her, Efu. A former student and one of the seventy-plus Somatic Experiencing (SE) trainers currently teaching my work around the world. I am eternally grateful to Efu and her colleagues as they respond to the call to heal. They are the future of SE. *Courtesy of Efu Nyaki.*

Plate 20. Dear, precious child.
I hold you in my heart.

At the time of the class, there was absolutely no mention of World War II, and certainly no one referred to the Nazis or the SS. I quickly learned there was an almost unwritten law that this subject was verboten, forbidden to acknowledge or speak about.

Much of the training I taught was about the energy and complexes we store in our bodies. As part of the course, students practiced many of the body awareness exercises we learn in Somatic Experiencing. I was demonstrating these sensate tracking tools with one of the students when I noticed how her body seemed to collapse in a specific way that I understood to be about shame. After getting her permission, I gently but firmly placed my hand on her shoulders and then slowly helped her to move into and out of the collapse, and back toward a more extended, uplifted posture of pride and dignity. After some moments of stillness, tears formed in her eyes, and then she cried unreservedly.

When she was ready, I asked if she was willing to talk about what she was experiencing. Another wave of tears overcame her. She then described her piercing shame about her father's involvement with Hitler's SS troops. Other students recounted similar feelings of shame for their own parents' or grandparents' involvement. Then another group of students opened up about their sorrow for their parents and family members who had been tortured or killed in the underground resistance. As both groups divulged their pain, a shared grief emerged. And in their shared grief was born a nascent healing bond, not only for them, but for me as well. As I continued to teach there, my fear dissolved as my generational trauma from the Holocaust was healed—the trauma that had caused my grandmother Doris to take her life by violent suicide.

As I got to know more about the German people, I developed a deep respect and even admiration for their culture. There was, of course, the extraordinary galaxy of admirable writers, poets, philosophers, and composers of old. But I also found the current Germans to be to be earnest, industrious, creative, and intellectually open, while also being rigorously attentive to detail. They were diligent students, and several of them later became teachers of my healing work, in various parts of Europe.

After the class had completed, I spent a few additional days getting to know Munich. I walked around the three-arched Victory Gate, the Siegestor, and appreciated the renewed levity and brightness of the city. However one day when I was walking near the Siegestor, I had a vision of red flowing down the external staircase of a building across the street. I shared this image with a German colleague, and he explained that this had been the site of a mass execution of students who were part of the resistance. The image I had seen symbolized their spilled blood. Because of the healing that had occurred in my class, I was able to witness this intuited apparition without being thrust into anxiety and panic. I was slowly assimilating the old and the new, in a way that allowed forgiveness and a renewal of trust.

Most inspiring to me was the German students' capacity to show remorse and seek atonement. This is something we Americans have been unable to confront, both as historical slave owners and genocidal murderers of First Nations peoples and African Americans. Our own anti-Semitic legacy continues to live on with little insight being directed toward it. We also face the virulent reemergence of white nationalism and white supremacy. As a society we Americans have been very weak in addressing these extreme ruptures to our moral integrity. I find that in our culture, the trauma continues to reverberate, often as an implicit bias that further diminishes our interconnection with fellow citizens. The capacity to move from individual healing to community and societal healing challenges each and every one of us. The world has much to learn from how the Germans have continued to address their collective shame and complicity. I do not mean to imply that they are paragons of virtue, but rather that they have sincerely and honestly tried to move their guilt into positive action.

My Own Racial Bias

With true embarrassment, I recall an episode when I personally demonstrated racial bias. The mayor of Los Angeles, Eric Garcetti, asked me to lead a training that dealt with the aftermath of child sex trafficking. In attendance were social workers, therapists, police, and sheriff deputies. After my workshop, a young Black woman came up to me and said she had gotten a great deal out of the training. She asked which of my books she should read to learn more about my methods. I reached in my bag and withdrew *Waking the Tiger*, my first book, and offered it to her, thinking it would be the simplest read. We continued our conversation, and I asked her about her current interests. I learned she had just received a doctorate in psychology and was now pursuing a law degree—all in her mid-twenties! I quickly realized that my stereotyping and implicit bias had led me to expect she would be new to the topic, and thus I had suggested the easier read. So, with great embarrassment, I reversed course and offered to give her some of my more complex books on trauma, *In an Unspoken Voice* and *Trauma and Memory*. It is with warmth and humility that I now recall this interaction. I was graced by her affording me this lesson in implicit bias, all without aggravating my shame about my inappropriate assumptions. She was clearly a new healer teaching the old guard, me!

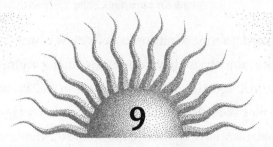

9

The Four Most Important Women in My Life

(Plus One Fiery Undergrad Student)

I have received gifts beyond measure from four powerful women: Charlotte Selver, Magda Proskauer, Ida Rolf, and Mira Rothenberg. Each of these pioneers has inspired my development as a professional, as a teacher, and as a person.

When I arrived at UC Berkeley from the University of Michigan in 1964, I simply didn't know I had a body. I was so alienated from it that I was essentially all mind, all in my head! "What else is there?" I wondered, alongside my fellow intellectuals. "Why do I even need to know I have a body?"

I first met Charlotte Selver in 1965 at the magnificent St. Mark's Lutheran Cathedral, located at the top of O'Farrell Street in San Francisco. I was spending two days at a workshop taught by Selver and her husband, Charles Brooks. The workshop was primarily offered to the Zen monks from the Green Gulch Farm Zen Center in Marin County, California, and the Tassajara Zen Mountain Center near Big Sur. But somehow my friend Jack Kaplan had successfully secured me a spot in this esoteric workshop.

A few words about Charlotte Selver: She was a force to be reckoned with, and must have done something right, as she lived and taught until age 102. In fact, as the story goes, when she was a ninety-six-year-old widow, she eloped with her fifty-year-old gardener, and apparently they lived happily ever after. See plate 8 and plate 9 for photos of my mentor Charlotte.

We began our class with this enigmatic lady by doing the most stupid, aggravating, and maddening exercises. For example we would pick up a stone and hold it in our hands, noting its size, shape, texture, temperature, and weight. This exercise seemed to go on forever. And when we did it with our eyes closed, it became somewhat disorienting. Then, even more difficult, with stone in hand, we walked around in circles. This went on for hour after miserable hour. We were instructed to notice how our feet contacted the ground. Which part of the foot touched the ground first, toes or heels, and which side made greater contact with the ground, inner or outer arches? Then she invited us to explore how our feet were connected with our ankles, and so on, up through our whole body. Finally, as we circled the room, I caught the eye of one of the monks and asked him what he was learning. His response: "I have a big headache." Finally someone was making sense!

Toward the end of the day, Charlotte Selver had us lay on our backs and told us to feel our breath coming in and out all the way from our feet, as well as other parts of our bodies. From a scientific perspective, I knew this didn't make sense and was frankly ridiculous; it was simply not possible. However at the end of the day, as Jack and I walked out of the church and looked down on the city valley and across to the bay bridge, everything became alive. Together we shared a vision of the city lights, scintillating in beautiful, harmonious synchrony. The only time I had experienced anything like this was when I took LSD. What acid did for me, I could do for myself: my living, sensing body could arrive at the same place, all by asking the right questions. But how to cultivate this level of body awareness? That inquiry led me to the breathing therapy of Magda Proskauer.

Magda Proskauer: Skating to Breathe

After my initial "awakening" with Charlotte Selver, I found my way to a little-known physiotherapist named Magda Proskauer. In a classic San Francisco Victorian house, perched above the hippies of the Haight-Ashbury, was her welcoming home and office. Her breathing therapy used the breathing function, at times combined with certain small movements, as a tool for the achievement of greater self-awareness. With her guidance over the course of the next year or two, I learned to experiment with my breath and to gradually become conscious of obstructing influences on spontaneous breathing.

My workshop with Charlotte Selver took many hours of concentrating on the body to evoke this lived connection. With Magda's breath-awareness, however, my inner expansion came more readily. In addition to being a physiotherapist, Magda was also a Jungian analyst. Sometimes an image would emerge when giving attention to my breath. At other times, we began our session by focusing on a recent dream and then finding its counterpart in the body. Magda's therapy helped me unify mind and body through images, sensations, and feelings. And during certain meetings, Magda would speak to me about her insights and theories.

Because of my scientific interests, she would sometimes schedule me at 11:30 a.m. so we might have time, after my session, to speak informally. We talked about her methods, and on occasion she would share intimate details of how she first came to therapy work.

At one of these meetings, she shared with me the story of how she became "awakened" to her body. As a young child during the cold European winters, she would skate on a frozen lake near her home. While figure skating one day, she felt a sensation like time evaporating, which gave rise to an awareness of "timeless flow." It was enlivening, and its imprint remained with her throughout her life. As a university student, however, Magda had to apply all her will to her academic studies, so she became temporarily disconnected from her sensing, knowing body. I think she shared all this with me as a way of helping me understand how I was also abandoning my body in the service of academic graduate studies.

Back to Magda's story. After graduation she received her physical therapy training at the University of Munich in Bavaria, Germany. There, using different forms of conventional breathing therapy, she treated patients with polio, cerebral palsy, and asthma. Some of these patients were cured, seemingly miraculously, and their recoveries were long-lasting. However, with other patients, even though they had quick improvements, their problems would reoccur.

Next, Magda began noticing whether the patients' breathing would become spontaneous during therapy sessions, and in particular whether their exhalation would become full and complete. In addition, she observed that their inability to exhale fully and naturally was linked to various psychological disturbances. In this regard, she immersed herself in the work of Carl G. Jung. She realized the act of breathing occupied a unique position as a bridge between conscious and unconscious processes. For example we can deliberately hold our breath or increase the rate of breathing. But we are rarely able to voluntarily modify autonomic functions such as our heart rate or blood flow. Thus through breath awareness, we are uniquely able to join conscious and unconscious processes. In this regard, for Magda, breath became the link between Jung's "collective unconscious" and conscious awareness, between mind and body, between Psyche and Soma.

Caught between Two Worlds

When I returned to the world of science, I was caught between my powerful experience of the workshop with Charlotte Selver and my breathing sessions with Magda Proskauer. I felt a pressing need to understand the science of what was happening in my body and nervous system during these sessions. Obviously something powerful was occurring when I felt the breath coming into my feet and other parts of my body, yet basic physiology clearly precluded our entire bodies from breathing.

As part of my monthly graduate stipend at Berkeley in 1965, I was entrusted with designing and teaching a laboratory-based undergraduate physiology class called Contemporary Natural Science (CNS). This class was bankrolled by the National Institutes of Health (NIH) to promote the teaching of natural science at the university level.

Plagued by the paradox between feeling and empirical facts, I had an idea. But first I needed a volunteer. A fiery, redheaded undergraduate student offered to stay after class and allowed me to connect her to several different electrical transducers. That way I could measure various physiological parameters and see if there was a correlation between those measures and breath. To record her breathing, I asked her to place a strain gauge around her lower chest. This measured her diaphragmatic breathing. I then connected

EMG (muscle electrical activity) electrodes to the bottoms of her feet. Next I recorded her heartrate with an EKG (an electrical heartbeat). Finally, I fastened a plethysmograph to one of her fingers to record changes in blood flow.

My thinking was that there might be an objective, measurable correlation between breath, muscle activity, heart rate, and blood flow. With all the aforementioned transducers connected, I watched the squiggles on a lie-detector-like recording device. But there was little on the way of correlation or covariance. They seemed randomly related. So, absurdly, I tried to guide my student the same way Charlotte Selver and Magda Proskauer had guided me. This led only to mutual frustration. But in a moment of shared irritation, there was an apparent breakthrough: I noticed that each time she drew a breath, there seemed to be a very slight increase in electrical activity in her muscles, presumably along with a minute muscle contraction. There was also an increase in heart rate and a decrease in blood flow to her finger. And conversely, when she breathed out, her muscles seemed to relax slightly, as well as a measurable decrease in heart rate, and a noticeably increased blood flow to her finger. Her breath then appeared more spontaneous, relaxed, and full.

When I asked my fiery volunteer to describe what she was experiencing, she barked, "Don't bother me!" Naturally my test subject was reluctant to emerge from her reverie and engage her intellect. However during a later discussion, it became clear she had entered a state of "flow," most likely similar to what I had undergone with Charlotte and Magda, or what Magda had felt during her childhood ice skating.

When I spoke to Magda, she seemed fascinated by what I had done in the laboratory with my volunteer subject. From this point forward, the blending of science and the healing arts became a guiding light in my professional and personal development.

The Iron Lady

I first met Dr. Ida Rolf in 1969. At the time, I was in my midtwenties and weighed about 130 pounds. She would sometimes refer to me, affectionately, as the young man with "a bag of bones and a waft of hair." Though I was both the slightest and youngest of her students, she miraculously agreed to train me in her method, called Structural Integration, or simply Rolfing.

For some reason she took a liking to me, perhaps because of my scientific mind, and even allowed me to occasionally call her "Grandma." Everyone else, with the exception of a colleague named Peter Melchior, was refused this familiarity. One evening she welcomed me as a guest in her Upper Manhattan apartment. After a lively discussion, she invited me to a local Jewish deli for dinner. She went on about how lucky I was to have a special relationship with her, while I nodded tentatively in agreement. As we finished our meals and walked toward the exit, an elderly Jewish couple speaking in thick Yiddish accents said to her: "Oh, you're so lucky to have such a lovely grandson." To this, she shrugged and offered me a faint smile. See plate 10.

The following year, I embarked on a ten-week study with her in Big Sur, California.

A Reckoning

On day one, Dr. Rolf waxed elegantly on her unique theories of the human body and shared some stories about the varied philosophies and approaches to phenomenology she had studied throughout her life.* The grand lady, adorned with a fresh gardenia nestled in her silver hair, then displayed her structural method of deep tissue manipulation on her chosen demonstration subject. The next day, once we had assembled in her living room, she asked us what needed to be done for the second of the ten sessions. We students trembled in fear of getting the wrong answer and being humiliated by her fierce requirements. To avoid suffering this fate during every class, we cornered two trained Rolfers, Peter Melchior and Jan Sultan, who lived in the Big Sur environs. We enticed them by buying them beers at the Esalen bar in exchange for their knowledge about the "recipe" for the next session.

So, on that fateful second morning, Dr. Rolf stood her model in front of the class—dressed only in his underpants, as was done in those days—and firmly challenged us to inform each other of what needed to happen next. One after another, we students recited the formulaic information we'd gotten from the two Rolfers the night before. Then, one after another, we were shot down in rapid succession. Finally, in exasperation, Dr. Rolf cried, "No! What do you see?" And again, "No, No, No! *What do you see?!*"

To See or Not to See, That Is Perception

In the months prior to studying with Dr. Rolf, one of my Berkeley lab mates, Earl Mehari, bequeathed me the use of a cabin in Bodega

---

*One particularly inspiring title she mentioned was the 1937 book by Mabel Elsworth Todd called *The Thinking Body*, which Dr. Rolf held in high esteem. Mabel Elsworth Todd is considered the founder of what has come to be known as Ideokinesis, a form of somatic education that became popular among dancers and health professionals in the 1930s.

Bay near where Alfred Hitchcock's horror movie *The Birds* was filmed. The rent for this small cabin, owned by a local fishing family, was fifteen dollars per month. On a small bookshelf rested a thin book with the succinct title *The Tide Pools of the Central California Coast*. Its pages depicted creatures living in the tidal pools. With this booklet in hand, I headed across the dunes at low tide and sat by a tide pool carved in the rocks. I looked into the pool, but even straining my eyes, I saw nothing. I checked the book again, thinking maybe it applied to a different California latitude. Finally, in near desperation, rather than staring at the tide pool, I gazed out to the horizon. I felt my eyes relax into the joining of sea and sky. As I opened to this sensation, I became more aware of the periphery of my vision. And to my surprise, without trying, I started to see little creatures darting back and forth in the tide pool. I gradually cultivated my newly emerging "soft seeing," a perception that has served me well to this day. As I became aware of what my body was doing as my vision changed, I realized I had relaxed the muscles in the back of my neck and skull. I was once again deeply grateful to Charlotte Selver for introducing me to body awareness. My takeaway lesson was that to see without effort, to truly see, unencumbered by the filters of the conscious mind, is to see things nakedly as they really are.

Back to Ida Rolf and that tense morning. Once more, she exclaimed, "What do you *see?!*" (Not "What do you think?") And in that delicate moment, as we all froze in anticipation, my vision shifted from straining to soft seeing. I was then able to describe the complex relationships between various parts of her model's body, and to communicate to the class as to whether his body movements and structure were coherent, or disorganized and disjointed. Finally, I could perceive how the whole was much greater than the sum of its parts. I observed an emergent property of the living body, "the web without the weaver." I was becoming an ethologist, before I really knew about them—though I would later learn to greatly admire their raw observational skill, which has served me well throughout my career.

A final debt of gratitude I owe to Dr. Rolf: she personally encouraged me to work with children and infants. See plate 11.

Mira: An Unexpected Reunion

In 1973 I was teaching my Berkeley students about the significance of our earliest memories, implicit traumatic imprints that occur in utero and during the perinatal period. The next week, one of my students brought in a library book written by a woman named Mira Rothenberg, titled *Children with Emerald Eyes*. I was deeply moved by her case studies. Two in particular stood out to me—more on that below. Mira writes from her gut, heart, and soul, not just from her intellect, though her mind is as sharp as that of anyone I know. In this book she delves below the complex anguish of her young patients and bequeaths us a gift beyond measure.

At the risk of sounding too mystical, when I first met Mira Rothenberg in 1975, I had the impression I had known her all my life; that in her, I had found a teacher and a soulmate. It was as though I'd discovered a missing part of myself. I first encountered Mira in person at her Brownstone house at 160 State Street in Park Slope, a few blocks from the Brooklyn Bridge. See plate 12. At that initial meeting, I was aware I had come face-to-face with a formidable force of nature. Mira, though utterly fierce, also had a rare capacity to join with a vulnerable child in their deepest place of hiding, and to gently coax them back from their terrifying abyss of isolation. She was able to slowly make contact with them and help them come out of their highly guarded citadel, one they had erected to protect themselves from a world too confusing, overwhelming, or cruel.

Even when Mira's book discloses one of her clinical failures, her candor about her persistent struggle in the face of insurmountable odds puts us in contact with our own deepest fears, hopes, and vulnerabilities. With these usually well-defended feelings revealed, we become unexpectedly strengthened by Mira's unfaltering, outstretched arm. These stories of transformation, failure, and triumph inspire courage in facing the darkest night of the soul. They are stories of pain and despair, of hope and resurrection, and finally, simply of our shared humanity. Here, I will touch on two of those stories.

Jonny

Jonny, "the incubator baby," was "one of the smallest baby boys ever to survive in the United States," weighing only one and a half pounds at birth. Mira describes how "his skin [was] shriveled and burned chocolate brown."[1] He was, by all accounts, "strangely ugly."[2] Unable to speak or walk, and apparently deaf and dumb, he was unreachable and unlovable. Jonny existed but did not live. Yet step by halting step, Mira was able to help him by breathing life into his limp and listless body, and then supporting him in taking his first steps, stabilized by her outstretched arms.

After many of their sessions together, Jonny developed a compulsion to get in front of the light bulbs in Mira's office. From the very start, Mira was struck by Jonny's tremendous preoccupation with lights. The brighter the light, the more strongly he was attracted to it, and the more he wanted to get close to it. Like a moth drawn to a flame, he would crawl directly under the brightest lights, while flapping his arms in a wing-like motion.

Jonny's fascination with lights seemed meaningful to Mira. She felt it should be pursued. So Mira had Jonny's father, a carpenter by trade, build a life-size replica of Jonny's incubator. He constructed it with several lights in a transparent box and brought it into Mira's house the night before Jonny's next session. In it they placed a doll that was same size Jonny had been when he was an incubator baby. The next day his parents brought Jonny to Mira's door and left him with her. The lights of the incubator were on as Jonny walked into the room. He sighted it immediately and stopped short. His whole body stiffened, and then trembled and shook, as his face turned an eerie "green."[3]

Then came the decisive moment. Jonny seemed to reel backward; yet instead of falling, he turned to Mira, and within a split second his face took on a look of anguish, rage, and accusation. It seemed to say, "How could you do this to me?" Mira recounts his reaction and notes how this was the first time his eyes actually focused on her—or, for that matter, on anyone. It took all Mira's strength to remember she *had* to be "brutal" to Jonny, confronting his trauma by exposing him to the incubator, for the sake of his healing.[4]

Within a few minutes Jonny became a different child. No longer was his face blank. It expressed feelings. For the first time Mira saw Jonny intact, emotionally and physically. She realized an important part of the battle had been won. When his mother came to pick him up, Jonny spoke the word "Mama," as he wept with her for the first time. Then, during subsequent treatment sessions, he broke down and sobbed bitterly. After this it became possible for him to cry. And along with daring to cry, he began to laugh, often heartily, and with a mischievous sense of humor. After three years of therapy with Mira, he cried when hurt, laughed when happy, loved and evoked love in others. He was gradually able to form relationships with other children and also with adults. He learned to consciously manipulate people and was adept at this in a way that was far beyond his years. He had become an altogether bright and engaging youngster.

Peter

Mira began this chapter, of my namesake, with these evocative images:

> *The antelope, the deer, and the gazelle are playing in the tall grass. The little chimpanzee is looking from the tree, enviously, curiously, at the whole terrain. . . . The newly born colt is testing the strength of his legs—still within his mother's reach, but already longing for the moment of freedom.*[5]

Needless to say, her reference to animal behavior triggered an intense and undivided attention in me, given my fascination with ethology. In addition, this chapter titled "Peter" prompted a surprising and almost reflexive identification. As I read through the pages that dealt with this autistic patient, I found my own inner wounding unexpectedly exposed by her deft prose. With these primal hurts laid bare, and with my imagining of Mira's presence, I was guided toward opening to my deepest Self. And you, dear reader, might also find that her astute renderings touch you, affecting your most private recesses and vulnerabilities.

Peter, the child in this chapter, had never known freedom. He was a little boy who, in contrast to Jonny, could walk and talk, and

occasionally laugh and cry. Peter would startle you with his phenomenal genius. He was a savant whose intellectual prowess sur-
passed the comprehension of many. As Mira describes, "From the
age of two, he could add, subtract, multiply, and divide numbers of
astronomical proportions," and, "By the age of seven he could do all
the crossword puzzles in the *New York Times* perfectly."[6]

Mira writes: "Peter was a little boy who was desperately and
irrevocably afraid of destruction. And since destruction seemed ever
present, he built himself a world where he alone, the master and
creator of it all, would reign in absolute power, and thus control
and circumvent his ultimate destruction."[7] Peter's solution to this
all-consuming terror was to deposit parts of himself throughout his
"kingdom." This allowed him to function, even though he was broken into pieces. Mira goes on to say, "His was a strange world, a very
lonely, frightening world; a very rigid, cruel world. . . . To appease
the gods of destruction, always lurking in prey for his life, he would
destroy himself."[8] These drastic survival tactics were the only choices
he could imagine. His story reminded me of when, as a child, I had
compulsively prayed to ward off my terror of being raped and abandoned again.

And thus Peter "lived in this strange world where danger lurked
all over and destruction was all around; but Peter, through a magic
of his own, escaped his fate. And everything he did in his world
was directed toward his one goal—survival."[9] He could not be alone;
it was simply too frightening, or too painful. And yet he was also
unable to connect to any other person. He could not coexist because
the dangers of obliteration were too great. Either aloneness or the
presence of others might bring disaster, terror, and endless pain.
"So," Mira writes, "in order to exist he ran from one to the other
within his terrifying labyrinth. Either weeping in hopeless want

and desperation, or shrieking in limitless, unspeakable agony, terror, and pain. . . . Since most of Peter's energies went into avoiding destruction, while denying any true living, there was little left for anything else; and thus the child gave the appearance of being feebleminded."[10] Mira also reflected that "He seemed a lonely dancer on a tightrope—always wobbly but desperately trying to maintain his balance. Not looking up or down, or anywhere around, for fear of losing his foothold, his hold on life. . . . Every ounce of energy was needed for the long and frightful dance."[11]

Mira's therapy with Peter extended over ten years, and his progress was often faltering, only occurring in tiny, step-by-step increments. And yet with Mira's outstretched hand and guidance, he learned to face his terrors and was able to gradually inhabit his body. I identified with Peter's struggle, connecting it to my own loneliness and terror. As described in previous chapters, I also learned to face my annihilation, sometimes with the use of psychedelics.

Mira's presence and mentorship taught me so very much. I was able to participate in her work with highly disturbed children at her inner city school in Brooklyn, and at Camp Blueberry in upstate New York. Mira had an unassuming yet potent capacity to engage these deeply disturbed children, many of whom were psychotic, schizophrenic, or autistic. This unique power she possessed was unconstrained by any dogma. And her rare ability to connect to their secret inner worlds revealed a gift that, unfortunately, seems less and less available in these times of mechanized and pharmaceutical "quick fixes" for treating mental illness.

Perhaps her greatest gift to me was showing me how to trust the unity of my gut, heart, soul, and mind. She helped me to face my demons—just as she had done for Jonny and Peter. With Mira, I gained the ability to enter the depths of my darkness and to celebrate when light shone through the cracks. What follows is an exploration of the development of our personal relationship.

Mira was often blunt, but always authentic. For the final fifteen years of her life until her death at age ninety-three, I would spend the month of September with her in New York City. It was always a rewarding gift to land in her Brooklyn brownstone as I recovered from jetlag, and from my busy summer's worth of teaching in Europe.

During one visit, I arrived with a suitcase of dirty clothes. I used her basement washing machine without her explicit approval. When I mentioned I had used it, she growled and nearly bit my head off. I recoiled at her raw fury and withdrew, like a scolded five-year-old, into the guest bedroom on the third floor. Clearly her rage was not to be dealt with in that moment of intense attack.

Later on I noticed that Mira was reluctant to throw away any food in her refrigerator. Her poor assistants were too intimidated by her temper to dispose of these items. But it was clear these spoiled foods were the reason for her ongoing stomach problems. So I took it upon myself to throw away a three-week-old batch of chicken soup. This prompted another volley of enraged words from Mira. However, unlike with the washing machine debacle, this time I stood my ground and calmly yet firmly commanded: "Mira, I won't let you poison yourself, not on my watch!" And suddenly her face relaxed and tears formed in her eyes, as her protective armor fell away.

I could see she was letting me touch a raw nerve, a deeply vulnerable wounding. This was her place of feeling rejected, unloved, and forsaken. She shared with me that as a child, her parents had fled Lithuania and escaped the Nazis by traveling to the United States. However, ten-year-old Mira was left behind with an unknown neighbor who lived at the edge of a dense forest. She spent much of her childhood alone in those dark woods. I was deeply touched that Mira trusted me to take the hand of that hurt child and bring her back from the dark forest.

I could now understand her tendency to hoard food, a product of her experience as the abandoned child, one of the escaping "Forest Jews." Though she was famous for bullying her aides, she was able to respect my standing up to her ferocity in the name of loving and caring for her. I could also relate to her fear of starvation, as my family had confronted hunger with my father's imprisonment. This was a deep terror we both knew all too well.

After I turned the tables on her, we became the best of friends and shared our journeys with each other. As far as the refrigerator went, we enjoyed fresh produce together, along with delicatessen items, particularly imported Jarlsberg cheese from Norway. To quote Friedrich Nietzsche, "I would believe only in a god who knows how to dance." Mira was a professional dancer in her youth, while in her mature years she was a magical spirit dancer, a healing sorceress.

Peter's strategy of hiding parts of himself throughout his domain recalls the compelling Egyptian myth of Isis and Osiris. Osiris was a great and beloved king who ruled Egypt, taught agriculture, and gave his subjects the rule of law and the roots of civilization. However Osiris's brother Seth was extremely jealous of him, so he killed Osiris and cut his body into pieces. He buried these parts throughout the kingdom, where they would be hidden for eternity. Yet Osiris's beloved consort, Queen Isis, out of deep love for her husband, searched the kingdom and found all of the hidden pieces. By bringing them back together, she "re-membered" him and thus made him whole again.

As for myself, I was also made whole by facing, again and again, my internal fragmentation and dissociation. Crucially, I did not do this alone, but with the presence and guidance of another. Trauma is not only what has happened to us; rather, it is what we hold inside in the absence of an empathetic, fully present witness.

I have incredible gratitude to Mira Rothenberg for meeting me where I was and allowing me to enter her world, as she entered mine. Thank you, big sister.

The Fruit Falls Close to the Tree: A Most Treasured Son

Mira had a son named Akiva (Kivie for short). I met him briefly as a toddler, and then again as a youngster. Fast forward to 2002, when I was watching the Academy Awards, since Mira had told me her son was nominated for Best Adapted Screenplay for the extraordinary film *A Beautiful Mind*. He won, as did Ron Howard for Best Director and Jennifer Connelly for Best Supporting Actress—and most impressive of all, the film claimed the Oscar for Best Picture! In his acceptance speech Kivie thanked his mother and father for teaching him how to enter the realm of a deeply disturbed mind. I wept at the honoring of that lineage, and their collective wisdom. See plate 13.

What Mira did with her therapy and books, Kivie and the cast of *A Beautiful Mind* did by taking us into the mind and soul of John Nash. They humanized both the gifts and curses of his schizophrenic, yet beautiful, mind. I have seen the movie several times, and each time I have been touched by the depth of his screenplay, the brilliant acting, and the inspired directing. We follow the disintegration, and then the reintegration, of John Nash, until, as a wizened old man, he receives the Nobel Prize in Economic Sciences for his contributions to what is now called the mathematics of Game Theory.

Thus I offer my deepest respect and thanks to both mother and son, for the gifts they have bequeathed to all of us in our shared humanity.

My Karass

As I contemplate these four incredible women, and other mentors I've had along the way, I sometimes wonder why they have been so generous, why they chose to support my development and growth. I suspect my curiosity and quest for knowing had something to do with it. At the same time, I don't think my intellect or personality played much of a role; rather, these teachers connected with something essential to who I was inside, my "spirit." And, though I do not wish to sound too New Age, I believe there were unseen forces that brought me together with these mentors.

Thus in reviewing these significant encounters, I am very curious as to how and why I came to meet these powerful and influential women. Carl G. Jung wrote about what he called "synchronicities." These refer to seemingly chance events, places, or encounters with persons we meet along our way. When we open to these possibilities, we may discover the emergence of mysterious, hidden forces and unexpected meanings. In Kurt Vonnegut's 1963 breakthrough novel *Cat's Cradle*, a fictional religion called Bokononism is secretly practiced by the defiant people of the fictional Caribbean island of San Lorenzo. When any two Bokononist worshippers meet, they secretly rub the bare soles of their feet together. This is done to inspire spiritual connection—sole to soul, so to speak. In carrying out this ritual act, people are able to discover whether they belong to the same "karass." Karass, in the novel, refers to a network or group of people that, unknown to each other, are linked "to fulfill the will of God." Further, this shared effort is governed by mysterious forces that each person can never be fully aware of. These encounters are where true mystery and wonder reside.

We are all capable of tapping in to such possibilities. But it takes a degree of willingness, curiosity, and trust to notice and then explore these priceless opportunities when they arise. Sometimes these encounters may occur with people who seem to share little in common with us as individuals. However, some of those people may hold pieces of a grand puzzle. And as we progress along this journey and touch sole to soul, the overarching purpose of our chance meetings may become clearer and clearer. This certainly was the case for me with these four most important women in my life.

> We all tell ourselves all sorts of things to make sense of the past . . . so much so that our fabrications, if we tell them to ourselves often enough, become the truth . . . in our minds, and everyone else's.[12]

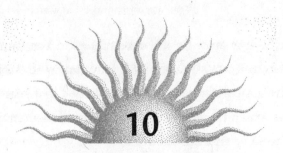

10

The Four Most
Important Men in My Life

It's all about energy.

P.A.L.

In all fairness to my gender, I wish to briefly acknowledge four important men in my academic, scientific life. Upon settling in to my doctoral work, teaching, and clinical practice in Berkeley in 1973, I was privileged to attend a postgraduate seminar in the biophysics department. This seminar was presented by an Israeli named Aharon Katchalsky, who studied the electrochemistry of biopolymer membranes. See plate 14. His landmark discoveries paved the way for the desalinization of ocean water, which was crucial to Israel's growth and sustenance. For this achievement he received many accolades and awards.

The complex mathematics of his equations were often over my head. However, I was able to discern the relevance of some of them. Fortunately I had the opportunity, on several occasions, to speak with this generous man about how his computations might be applied to some of my clinical observations.

Tragically, however, in 1974 Katchalsky was murdered in a terrorist attack at the Ben Gurion International Airport in Tel Aviv, in which twenty-six people were killed and scores of others were injured. Interestingly, in 1973 just before this catastrophe, his younger brother Ephraim Katchalsky—also a biophysicist by training—was elected president of Israel.

Order Out of Chaos

The flow of energy through a [complex] system
acts to organize that system.

HAROLD MOROWITZ, *ENERGY FLOW IN BIOLOGY*

Aharon Katchalsky's sudden absence left me with feelings of sorrow and emptiness. I missed our inspiring discussions. Fortunately, a friend of one of my lab mates, knowing of my interests and of my lost mentor, handed me a thin black book written by Ilya Prigogine, titled *An Introduction to Thermodynamics of Irreversible Processes.* This work, published in 1961, seemed to follow a similar track to that taken by Katchalsky in his own work. Prigogine was best known for his study of what he called "dissipative structures" and their role in thermodynamic systems—a discovery that won him the Nobel Prize in Chemistry in 1977. See plate 15. In brief, Ilya Prigogine discovered that the importation and dissipation of energy into complex chemical systems could result in the emergence of new, unexpected structures, due to internal self-reorganization. So what does all this really mean?

In physics, the second law of thermodynamics states that when you introduce energy into a physical system, that system becomes more and more disordered; this is called entropy. As a simple example, if you introduce energy—in the form of heat—to ice, the ice melts and becomes water. Water is less ordered than the crystalline structure of ice. And then if you continue to introduce energy—more heat—the water becomes vapor, a gas. The vapor molecules are much less ordered than the liquid ones, and liquid water is, in turn, less ordered than ice. This disordering is characteristic of a closed, "conservative" system, and is aligned with the second law of thermodynamics. In other words, the universe is going to hell in a hand basket. But not to worry! This process would take billions of years to make any real difference.

Dissipative Structures

Too much of anything is bad;
otherwise it wouldn't be too much.

NORMAN KRETZMANN

In contrast to closed systems, Prigogine studied dissipative structures. These relate to the structure of matter due to the organization of energy flow—shades of Einstein's relativity theory. A system, or structure, is said to be dissipative if it exchanges and disperses energy with its environment. A dissipative structure is a thermodynamically open system that is operating outside of, and often far from, thermodynamic equilibrium. It is embedded in an environment with which it exchanges energy and matter. And, I would add, with which it also exchanges information.

In contrast to entropy, Prigogine made the monumental discovery that under certain conditions, the introduction of energy into an open system could actually cause that system to shift to a higher level of organization, or in other words, to exhibit "negative entropy," the opposite of entropy. It would be like if water could reconfigure itself into ice crystals with the addition of heat, a contradiction to the second law of thermodynamics; an impossibility. Prigogine went on to realize that, given certain boundary constraints, this introduction of energy could actually lead to "internal self-reorganization." And this is exactly what I had been observing in my students and clients: That if I carefully, slowly introduced them to gently touching or "titrating" their traumatic sensations, emotions, and images, they would then enjoy greater stability, clarity, and forward direction in their lives; in other words, something like negative entropy. However if too much energy was introduced into such a metastable system, or if the energy was introduced too rapidly, the system would likely degrade into disorder and be potentially retraumatizing.

It was my observation and hypothesis that positive transformation only occurred if the nervous system was stimulated enough to make a change in the system, yet at the same time not overstimulated; in other words, if certain boundary constraints were adhered to. Clinically, I had observed that exposure to any trauma-related sensations, emotions, or images needed to be gradually titrated, one step at a time, for positive transformation to reliably occur. I held the belief that certain therapies, which depended on continual emotional release and abreaction, could in fact be overloading the nervous system, especially the autonomic nervous system (ANS), thus leading to further disorganization and decompensating regression.

Therefore, my next step was to envision how the theory of dissipative structures could guide me in understanding when gradual re-exposure would likely promote therapeutic progress, and when it could potentially hinder it. To solve this problem, I looked to the work of mathematician René Thom on catastrophe theory.

A Beautiful Catastrophe Fold

At a time when so many scholars in the world are calculating, is it not desirable that some, who can, dream?

RENÉ THOM

One more piece to this puzzle was needed to make it clinically relevant. This was the work of the brilliant French mathematician René Thom, who developed catastrophe theory. René Thom inspired me when he wrote, "At a time when so many scholars in the world are calculating, is it not desirable that some, who can, dream?"[1] I also delighted in the playful quality of his photo portrait and could easily imagine him tossing bright ideas back and forth with his intellectual friends at a Parisian café. See plate 16.

Catastrophe theory is a mathematical method for describing the evolution of forms in nature. It was invented by René Thom in the 1960s. Thom expounded the philosophy behind the theory in his innovative 1972 book, *Structural Stability and Morphogenesis*. There, he demonstrated that catastrophe theory is particularly applicable where gradually changing forces produce sudden, abrupt effects. The extension of his theory has been successfully applied in the social and biological sciences by E. C. Zeeman. As Zeeman proposed, things that change suddenly, by "fits and starts," have long resisted mathematical analysis. His method derived from the topology of seven "elementary catastrophes." The key that I derived from this work was that small shifts in the autonomic nervous system could have great effects on behavior, such as attack and fear, and that when these behaviors could in turn be altered, by slight changes, the autonomic nervous system balances.

So, while the four women—Selver, Proskauer, Rolf, and Rothenberg—inspired me to connect with my alive, sensing body, Prigogine (coupled with Katchalsky) and Thom (coupled with Zeeman) inspired me academically and scientifically. Their work prompted me to take a graduate course in quantum chemistry to help me along the way. Thus I learned to hold together these important polarities: the feeling, lived world on the one hand, and the quest for scientific knowledge and intellectual clarity on the other. Together, their dialectic supported my development as a scientist, clinician, teacher, and a person with a life's mission.

Artificial Neuron Project: Leon D. Harmon

In my sophomore year at the University of Michigan, around 1961–62, I attended a guest lecture by a researcher named Leon D. Harmon, who worked at Bell Labs in Murray Hill, New Jersey. At the time, pure research was carried out at that lab by a number of renowned scientists, including a few Nobel Prize winners. These included the discoverer of the background radiation noise from the "Big Bang" at the birth of the universe, as well as the inventors of the transistor and the laser.

Bell Labs also housed other pure scientists, including Leon Harmon, a largely self-taught electrical engineer. Harmon had fashioned a small circuit board with five transistors that were connected in such a way as to simulate the electrical behavior of a single nerve cell, called a neuron. These parameters included excitatory and inhibitory inputs that represented the analog behavior of synapses, the chemical connection between neurons. Then the "all or nothing" propagation of a nerve impulse along the cell axon was also simulated by the artificial neuron. What Harmon did was to connect a few these artificial neurons together in networks based upon known simple invertebrate neuroanatomy. He would then see if he could predict new physiological findings. He managed to do this successfully for the compound eye of the Atlantic horseshoe crab (*Limulus polyphemus*). This simulation was based on the electro-physiological experiments of Michael (Michelangelo) Fuortes and Keffer Hartline, who received a Nobel prize in physiology for discovering how that simple eye detected edges. As an aside, I later had the opportunity to visit both Hartline and Fuortes, the archetypes of the modest and generous scientists, working at the Marine Biological Laboratory in Woods Hole, Massachusetts.

The Michigan lecture by Leon Harmon took place at the home of Spike Tanner, where I fortunately worked part time. When Harmon had finished speaking, I was barely able to contain my excitement and immediately plied him with a multitude of questions. Every fiber of my being secretly yearned to have him as a mentor and to work with him on modeling these neural networks; to live my life as a student of "neuro-cybernetics." I must confess, with more than a shade of blushing embarrassment, that at the time, I believed from my academic studies that our brains were essentially machines, albeit complex ones, but machines nonetheless. I thought if we could understand the mechanisms of the brain, we would be able to comprehend all our behaviors, perceptions, and even our very motivations. I thought of the brain as being akin to a black box. Once we knew what was inside the box, we could then, like the artificial neurons, predict what response would happen for any given stimulus: a clear causal chain of Stimulus → Black Box → Response.

A month or so after the lecture, I received a surprise letter from the Bell Labs. As I ran home to my off-campus room, I ripped it open, almost tearing it in half. The letter was from Leon Harmon, offering me a fellowship to spend the coming summer working with him in his lab. Not only that, but I was also to receive a $250/month stipend for my living expenses—which at the time was quite adequate. I was in heaven! By the end of the summer, I was convinced I had found my direction in life.

About ten years after this fellowship, I began developing the rudimentary theory behind my evolving stress-trauma healing method. In doing so, I was confronted by the dilemma between the concept of human brains as machines, or the algebraic sum of their neuron parts, versus the idea of the human mind as a phenomenon exhibiting a degree of complexity that cannot be predicted by adding up its individual components. During this time, I came across a small book written by the preeminent physicist Erwin Schrödinger, titled *What Is Life?* He reasoned that the laws of biology should be explainable by applying the fundamental laws of physics. This delightful essay, published in 1952, describes a troubling paradox, one that seemed to haunt him throughout his later life: In this slim edition, he puzzled over why biological life seemed, clearly, to move to higher levels of order, while the second law of thermodynamics in physics predicted disorder and disintegration, or in other words, increasing entropy. For this puzzling paradox, the brilliant 1933 Nobel Prize recipient could find no explanation.

So then, what was it that propelled biological systems toward higher levels of order?

(My) Emergence

In contrast to the black-box, stimulus-response view of the brain and behavior, the theory of emergent properties differs in fundamental ways. It posits that rather than a living organism being simply the sum of its individual parts, the whole is much greater than the sum of these parts. Furthermore, such organisms develop organically according to principles of self-regulation and what are called emergent properties. Emergent phenomena manifest themselves as the result of various system components working together in nondeterministic ways. In other words, complex systems or collections of such systems exhibit the property of emergence, which their individual parts cannot come close to predicting.

One interesting example of emergent behavior comes from evolutionary biologist E. O. Wilson's meticulous study of the behavior of ant colonies. On its own, an ant behaves erratically, flailing about aimlessly with a small twig in its mandible, or mouth. It is unable to do anything useful with it, and seems incapable of exhibiting anything more than the simplest, most "mindless" random and repetitive movements, all without apparent purpose. The single ant is completely unable to correct and adapt its behaviors to its own needs or to changes in the environment. In jaw-dropping contrast, an ant colony accomplishes astounding tasks. These include building nesting hills and dams with twigs, as complex as those designed by some human engineers; finding and moving large amounts of food; and most fascinating, linking together to form a bridge across a body of water, allowing the single queen ant to safely traverse to the other side. All these are complex behaviors not remotely predictable by studying the individual behavior of a single ant or even small groups of ants. In this context, emergent properties are the purposeful changes that occur in ant behavior when individual ants work together in an unexpected and wondrous symphony.

Another example of emergent behavior comes from the study of the brain and nervous system. Human consciousness may well be called an emergent property of the nervous system. Like the ants that make up a colony, no single neuron, synapse, tract, or even nucleus holds information of sufficient complexity to resemble human self-awareness or emotions. Nonetheless, the sum of all neurons in the nervous system generates complex human behaviors and emotions like fear, sadness, and joy, none of which can be attributed to a single neuron or brain region. Many neurobiologists concur that the complex interconnections among the parts give rise to qualities that belong only to the whole. In my doctoral dissertation, published in 1976, I demonstrated that the nervous system exhibited complex properties and behaviors that could be represented by catastrophe theory, then a new branch of mathematics introduced by René Thom. Around this time, I had a dream:

I am walking toward what appears to be an elevator on the ground floor of a tall building. There is a tube like the shaft of an elevator. Within the tube sits a large sphere and at the center of the sphere is a door. As I walk toward the door, the hair on my neck stands up. I turn around and see Leon Harmon behind me, glaring with an expression of disgust and disapproval. I feel paralyzed. Part of me is drawn toward the door, but another part is apprehensive of going against Harmon, my mentor and father figure. In that fateful moment, I walk through the elevator door. I feel both relieved and terrified. I am on my own. Have I betrayed Harmon, or has he abandoned me? Or have *I* abandoned me?

Upon waking from the dream, I imagined myself again situated between Harmon and the elevator. I felt a powerful pull. I wanted desperately to enter the door, but I was also pulled back by Harmon's displeasure. Finally, I imagined entering the elevator. I watched the door slide closed, separating the two of us forever. My life was now moving in a very different direction, from below to above.

During the next few days, the meaning of the dream became increasingly clear. First I realized the building was quite tall, and the elevator I had entered was on the ground floor—the floor that rested on the building's foundation. The image of the elevator was a representation of the autonomic nervous system. The spherical swelling was like the autonomic ganglia, or clusters of nerve cell bodies, and the shaft represented the autonomic pathways connecting the human brain and body. This part of the nervous system encompasses the midbrain-diencephalon and upper brain stem, the brain regions associated with our instincts, as well as with homeostasis, the dynamic equilibrium state of our internal organs. This is also the sensation-based part of the nervous system. I realized that the "higher functions" of the nervous system were represented by the top stories of the tall building: functions such as intellect, perception, morality, and creativity. What my dream revealed, however, was that the building rested on a foundation that was the base for the entire structure.

As I was to understand it, these higher functions were actually emergent properties of the foundation, or "lowest level," of the autonomic nervous system, home to our core instincts and emotions. My understanding suggested that the brain stem, cerebellum, and autonomic nervous system formed the foundation, the so-called lowest part of the nervous system. And the tall edifice, representing our intellect, was built upon this basic matrix in the brain stem and cerebellum, from which we construct all that we feel and know about ourselves, and all we perceive about our world. Do we feel that the world is generally a safe place, or do we habitually perceive threats where they are not? These refined, complex conscious perceptions could also be considered emergent properties. In some way they resemble the complex behavior of ant colonies. This may be consciousness itself emerging from the billions of connections between simple neurons.

In other words, the most primitive portions of the brain and nervous system, as could be represented by the basement of a house, give rise to that which is above, to our very perceptions and feelings about the world. To quote the Kybalion again, "As above, so below; as below, so above." In terms of my own perspective, I was moving beyond seeing myself as only a mind, carried from place to place by a supposedly mechanical body, to realizing I had a sensing, feeling, instinctual, knowing body. In the words of the singer Dory Previn: *Curse the mind that mounts the clouds / In search of mythical kings / And only mystical things. . . . Cry for the soul that will not face / The body as an equal place / And I never learned to touch for real / Or feel the things, iguanas feel.* Here, in the body, in the home of the iguanas—that is where I want to live!

T. Berry Brazelton

The aforementioned men were important intellectual and academic mentors. In contrast, my fourth mentor was a wise physician, filled with feeling and warmth. He was my favorite mentor. His name was T. Berry Brazelton, and he was known in pediatric circles for his development of the Neonatal Behavioral Assessment Scale (NBAS), which is widely used to assess an infant's neurological development and its engagement with caregivers. Brazelton also hosted the 1983 cable television program *What Every Baby Knows*. This was a marvelous program, and one I rarely missed when I was at home. He showed how each infant is a unique being from day one.

In one episode, Brazelton referred to the parent and child "falling in love" with each other. The most important thing parents can do, he proposed, is to help develop bonding and attachment. To do this, one must become a careful observer of their child and learn to interpret their needs. I would suggest he was another ethologist, a keen observer of human behavior!

You can see the essence and passion of this man when he is holding, rocking, and caressing an infant as they unmistakably fall in love with each other; and I could not help but fall in love with Brazelton. While his work was radical fifty-plus years ago, his message was simply that a baby is already a whole human being, longing to engage with their caregivers and with the world. And through a joyful dance, a partnered tango, parent and baby can co-participate with each other in play, mirroring, and excitement.

My only contact with Brazelton was in written correspondence, through which I shared the work I was developing with babies and children who had survived birth or perinatal trauma as well as other childhood traumas. He was genuinely interested and supportive and sent me copies of his published articles. Some years ago, I was awarded a lifetime achievement award for my work with traumatized babies and children. With no intention of comparing myself to this gentle giant, I must admit I was beyond pleased to be recognized by the organization that had given Brazelton the very same award years before. I will forever hold his kindness and generosity of spirit in my heart. He understood the value of tenderness and attuned care, neither of which I had received as an infant.

When I first saw Brazelton on television in 1983, something twisted in my heart. On the one hand, I felt as if he were talking directly to me about my loss and despair as an infant. But on the other, he intensified my resistance to feeling that primal wound. His soft, welcoming presence provoked my earlier, reactive interest in behaviorism.

Let me review this interest, which started in my sophomore year at the University of Michigan in 1962. There, I was able to attend a graduate seminar in Skinnerian operant conditioning with a young, up-and-coming professor named Harlan Lane. Before Brazelton's time, the behaviorists held sway in child and infant care. They approached the subject without feeling, as if questioning how to raise an object rather than a human being. They saw a child as simply a thing to be conditioned with positive or negative reinforcement. Behaviorism was the theory that the behavior of animals and humans could be explained in terms of conditioning. This theory did not take thoughts or feelings into consideration. It suggested that psychological disorders were best treated by altering a child's behavior patterns using conditioning methods. Paradoxically, the behaviorists believed that conditioning, which had caused the problems in the first place, would somehow solve them—a bit of circular thinking at best.

John Watson, the grandfather of behaviorism, believed that children were tabulae rasae, or blank slates, and proclaimed, "Give me a dozen healthy infants. . . . and I'll guarantee to take any one at random and train him [in other words, condition him] to become. . . . a] doctor, lawyer, artist, merchant-chief and, yes, even beggar-man and thief, regardless of his talents, penchants, tendencies, abilities, vocations, and the race of his ancestors."* Watson believed that "children should be treated as 'small adults,'" and

---

*Note: "Tabula rasa is the theory that individuals are born without built-in mental content, and therefore, all knowledge comes from experience or perception. Its proponents disagree with the doctrine of innatism which holds that the mind is already born in possession of certain knowledge." ("About: Tabula rasa," *DBpedia*.) John Locke was the first to use the term *tabula rasa*. In his 1689 work "An Essay Concerning Human Understanding," he argues that the mind is a tabula rasa, or blank slate, which we fill with ideas as we move through the world.

shown emotional detachment. As such, he warned against the "inevitable dangers of a mother providing too much love and affection."[2] This paucity of affection was truly the antithesis of Brazelton's warm and supportive advice to parents. And in fact, my own upbringing was more or less shaped by this idea of not loving the child too much.

Watson famously raised his children according to his behaviorist principles. Yet notably, three of his four children—Mary, William, and James—attempted suicide. William eventually died of suicide in 1954 after a second attempt. So much for Watson's child-rearing theories and practices. Possibly some of his worldview was the result of having been raised on a poor, bleak farm in South Carolina, where he was abandoned by his father and probably did not receive frequent touch or affection from his mother.

Following in the footsteps of Watson, B. F. Skinner, another noted behaviorist, developed the concept of "operant conditioning." This is the idea that you can influence an animal's behavior in experiments by allowing it to manipulate an object such as a lever, in order to obtain a reward—or receive a punishment if it fails to press the lever at the right time. In my sophomore year at the University of Michigan in 1961–62, I was allowed to participate in a graduate psychology seminar on Skinnerian operant conditioning. As a special project, I trained a rat to carry out a daring rescue. I first conditioned my rodent subject to push a toy fire truck with an extended ladder along the floor of a "Skinner box." Next, with continued positive reinforcement, I conditioned the rat to climb the ladder, which now leaned against the far wall of the Skinner box. At the top of the ladder, sitting on a narrow ledge below a painted window, I positioned a small plastic baby. For additional effect I painted flames reaching up from the window. Finally, I conditioned the rat (step by step) to climb the ladder, take the baby in its mouth, and then gently bring it down to the ground.

For my eventual success, I would have to wait patiently and observe the rat's every movement. I would then shape its behavior by giving it a positive reward, some goodie treats, when it came anywhere near the desired part of the box. For example if it was in the area behind the fire truck, it got its first reward. Then, if it accidently nudged the fire truck, I would instantly give it another reward. And so this went on, piece by piece, until I linked together the entire sequence of pushing the engine, climbing the ladder, and finally "rescuing" the baby from the burning building. To the naive observer, this looked like one purposeful, intelligent movement sequence when in reality it was a series of piecemeal, reinforced rewards. The herculean task of training the rat in the full sequence took me two weeks to accomplish. When I finally demonstrated my achievement in front of the wide-eyed class, I received a standing ovation from the roomful of graduate students. So then why couldn't I believe in conditioning theory with such an apparent success under my belt?

Watson and Skinner both believed that one could alter or "shape" a baby's, toddler's, or preschooler's behavior with positive and negative reinforcement. In a chilling "experiment," Skinner actually raised his own daughter Deborah in a contraption similar to a Skinner box. A 1945 article in *Ladies' Home Journal* magazine featured a photograph of a child in this box. See plate 17. In the article Skinner says that when his second daughter, Deborah, was born in 1944, he'd built a crib of sorts that functionally resembled a very large hospital incubator. It was essentially a box with a door and a Plexiglas window to observe the newborn.

Skinner called his invention a "baby tender" and it gave Deborah a warm, comfortable place to sleep through the notoriously cold Minnesota winters. Skinner and his wife were particularly focused on reducing the amount of layers they'd need to wrap Deborah in, not only to give her more freedom of motion, but also to cut down on laundry. I'll also add that this prevented the baby from being exposed to human touch and holding. Deborah slept in this incubator-like crib of her father's design until she was two-and-a-half. It has been stated that, "By all accounts she had a healthy, happy childhood and adulthood."[3]

However, as she grew up rumors and stories circulated to the effect that, as a result of being raised in this box, she became psychologically damaged, sued her father, and then later attempted suicide. There seems to be considerable debate about the veracity of these stories. Apparently Deborah later denied these rumors and said she was loved by her father. However, traumatized children often exhibit what has been called a "fantasy bond." In other words, these people will manufacture love where it did not exist, just so they can feel loved. The only direct information I have on this matter comes from one of my lab mates in the Invertebrate Neurophysiology lab at Berkeley. She was Deborah's roommate at Radcliffe College and told me Deborah had been in and out of psychiatric institutions. Since I don't have any further direct information about Deborah, I will leave the matter here.

So, to add to Watson's list of conditioned, so-called "pliable" babies who later attempted or committed suicide, we might possibly add Skinner's troubled daughter Deborah. Here, it is useful to review Mira's therapy with Jonny, the incubator baby, left alone without touch or a parent's embrace. But the one data point that seems a robust indictment of the behaviorist approach to child rearing is the fate of Watson's deeply disturbed, suicidal children. So as an experiential exercise I urge you to consider plate 17 and plate 18. Notice what you experience in your body and mind as you look at each photo.

Truly, it took me decades to recognize and undo the personal damage of my own cold, unemotional, behaviorist upbringing. One exercise I undertook as a result of T. Berry Brazelton's welcoming warmth was to dare to imagine receiving nurturance in the form of warm, vanilla-flavored milk coming from a welcoming, full breast. I practiced visualizing this enlivening, archetypal feminine imagery for a year. Better late than never!

Honorable Mentions:
My Two Brothers from Other Mothers

The map may not be the territory,
But it sure as hell helps you to get around.

P.A.L.

Stephen Porges
When I first met Stephen Porges around 1975, I was in the thick of teaching my trauma healing work to a group of Berkeley therapists. Steve, by contrast, came from the stifling, ultra-competitive, and often vicious world of academia and research—the academic-industrial complex.

He was on leave from the University of Illinois to take a sabbatical year at UCLA. I flew down from Berkeley to LA, and we spent the day reveling in each other's company. Talk about a "karass"! At that meeting we became lifelong brothers in crime, a union of the "Berkeley Hippie" and the professorial academician. I told him about my physiology recordings and body awareness work, and he shared with me a measure of coherence that he had been developing, called "vagal tone." This measured the rhythm between breathing and heart rate. What I had blundered through in my experiments with the fiery redheaded student in my Berkeley laboratory, he was able to measure mathematically. But even more thrillingly, we both shared the vision of "emergent properties," a vision we would further develop during the decades that followed. Briefly, the concept of emergence is a way of characterizing life and its origin, which offers an alternative to reductive explanations of life. Porges would continue to follow this theme in 1994, when he introduced his landmark polyvagal theory.

In recounting our first meeting, I must defer to Stephen's amusing recollection of what transpired. He offered to pick me up at the LA airport, and I told him I would wear a red carnation prominently displayed in the lapel of my white sports jacket so that he could easily recognize me. Yet when he sighted me among the airport crowds, he was surprised to see this eccentric long-haired hippie accosted by a young damsel dispensing the Hare Krishna version of the Bhagavad Gita while loudly proclaiming, "God loves you and I love you!" Allegedly my response to this impassioned declaration was to sweep her up and plant a hearty kiss on her cheek, with the rejoinder, "I love you too!" She reversed direction and fled in apparent distress. Steve watched this odd display from a distance before tentatively approaching me. With some uncertainty and curiosity, we made our introductions before heading off to the UCLA campus, thus commencing our forty years of brotherly collaboration.

In methodically and painstakingly developing the polyvagal theory, which he first proposed in 1994, Porges gave therapists a clear map for tracking the internal states of their clients or patients, and effectively responding to any shifts therein. And as we two brothers of the heart have aged, this map has also shown us how to keep alive and in contact with our vitality so as to allow continued exploration and teaching. Thank you, brother, for our shared lives together.

Bessel van der Kolk

My other "brother from another mother" is Bessel van der Kolk, with whom I have engaged in a sometimes difficult (though also a genuinely caring) relationship. When we first met at a conference about the body in psychotherapy, in the early 1990s in Boulder, Colorado, he seemed dismissive. I think this defensiveness resulted from the fact that at the time, those of us participating in the conference were considered to be on the fringe of the psychiatric field. However, to his great credit, Bessel gradually explored the possibility that "the body keeps the score" when it comes to trauma. And in doing so, he courageously risked the wrath of his psychiatric colleagues.

For several years Bessel and I presented together at the Esalen Institute in the wilds of Big Sur, California. I think that these were exciting, rich, and collaborative times for both of us. Then, around 2006 we decided to write a book together. This attempt turned out to be difficult, but it was also a profoundly valuable exchange; and when we were about ready to "strangle" each other, we parted ways. In 2010 I published *In an Unspoken Voice: How the Body Releases Trauma and Restores Goodness*. Bessel, with coaxing from myself and others, eventually published his *New York Times* bestseller, *The Body Keeps the Score*. In a twist of fate, his books and lectures, as well as my own, have taken the body out of the fringe and brought it into the mainstream of psychotherapy. And, with unexpected humility and grace, he acknowledged that he shared the reason why we didn't get our book written together. But the richness of our collaboration (and genuine affection) inspired both of us and we stand together in our message to up-and-coming, and seasoned, therapists to put the body in its rightful place, to give the body its due. Thank you, brother, colleague, and friend. I hope that we will continue to grow and collaborate together, which started at our meetings on Long Pond, near Cabot, Vermont.

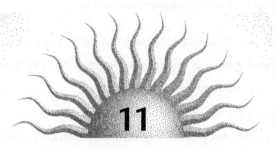

Reflections of an Unsuspecting Prophet

At this point in my life, Somatic Experiencing, the work I developed over fifty-plus years, is taught by about seventy trainers, to over fifty thousand therapists and healers in forty-four countries. So the weight now is shared on the collective shoulders of these many trainers all over the world. It has indeed taken a heavy load from my shoulders. The question is: What happens next? I do have a couple more books gestating. One I call *Trauma and Spirituality: Resilience and the Human Spirit*, written with my dear friend and colleague Mariana Bentzen; and the other, *Healthy Adolescent Sexuality: A Book for Parents and Their Teens*. This one I plan to write with my partner and longtime friend Laura Regalbuto.

During the past twenty-two years, Laura and I have been in each other's lives. It has not been a "traditional" childbearing relationship, though we have gestated much together, including this book. There is much we have agreed upon, while in other places we have been at odds; but we are gradually learning to accept those differences. We have evolved a growing fondness and appreciation for each other's strength and intellect and the sharing of art and music.

It has been very much of a learning and growing relationship. Both Laura and I have come to understand what it is to be in relationship, to communicate, to listen and to be heard; and we have learned that authentic contact is about accepting our differences.

My current intention is to gradually withdraw from my teaching, from being so much in the world, and to "retire." Yet fate doesn't seem to agree with this plan. Somehow, irrespective of my supposed goal of retirement, I continue to teach postgraduate classes internationally and do various interviews. I have become an unlikely and imperfect "prophet," a stranger in a strange land. Hopefully in completing this autobiography, I can go on to the next chapter of my life, welcoming whatever it may bring. Perhaps during this next phase of transition I can take some guidance from Efu.

Efu

While sitting across from Euphrasia Nyaki, I am thoroughly mesmerized by her extraordinary beauty, grace, and the strength of her gentle presence. Dressed in the colorful local garb of her Tanzanian tribal village, she exudes a luminous spirituality, grounded by an earthly inner authority. See plate 19. She had been tasked with interviewing me for an upcoming international conference. Captivated by her striking presence, I responded to her soft-spoken queries. We embarked on a spirited flow of conversation bolstered by our deep and authentic regard for each other.

Efu—her nickname—is a former student of mine. She now commands a well-deserved respect as an international trainer, teaching Somatic Experiencing in many developing and first-world countries. Being an African Catholic missionary has not stopped her from blending her traditional herbal medicine, and the ancestral tribal wisdom of her Nyaki clan, with her trauma healing work. In founding the AFYA healing center in subequatorial Brazil, she has offered her bright spirit and vibrant presence to humanity's wounds and their healing. Her authority is both rich and heartfelt. She is, incidentally, also a jaw-droppingly magnificent Afro-Brazilian dancer, even by the high standards of the sensuous, lively Brazilians.

Midway through our dialogue, Efu firmly but gently proclaimed: "Peter, you do realize you are a prophet?" Unnerved by this sudden declaration, I visibly retracted and struggled to respond. Again she said, with even more emphasis, "You are a prophet, a prophet for these troubled times, and you need to own that role!" When I let this unexpected word permeate into my wary reserve, I again recoiled with chagrin and self-doubt. But then I breathed cautiously into the challenge of owning that somber role, as Efu had so insistently instructed. Clearly, the student had become the teacher.

Words matter, so the idea of claiming that label and thus exposing myself to scorn scared the bejesus out of me. I thought, "What hubris, to even consider that I might have the qualities of a prophet!" I recalled the influential book by the spiritual philosopher Kahlil Gibran, titled *The Prophet*. This is a thin volume, though thick with poetic wisdom. So how could I possibly identify myself with this *real* prophet? In thumbing through a pocket edition, I came across this paragraph:

> Even your body knows its heritage and
> its rightful need will not be deceived.
> And your body is the harp of your soul,
> And it is yours to bring forth sweet
> music from it or confused sounds.

One anonymous Sufi writer was even more succinct: "The Body is the shore on the Ocean of Being." Though we may be unaware, we all stand on that shore. This autobiography explores the personal story of my journey in harnessing the living, knowing body in the healing and transformation of trauma. All my life I've explored this question of whether we can bring forth sweet music from our bodies out of the discordant cacophony of trauma. And I've found that, with the right tools and support, the choice is ours! So, whether I am a prophet or not, I do concur with these two wise mystics about the importance of enlisting the body in the healing and transformation of trauma.

Perhaps these mystics and I are ultimately cut from the same cloth in the tapestry of body/mind healing, and I am but a single thread in that wondrous fabric of understanding and wisdom. In that case I might qualify, in some small measure, as a minor "quasi-prophet." Either way, I have been gifted and graced with the opportunity to teach something that fills my soul with passion and fuels a fire in my belly, while allowing me to help heal humanity's wounds. This work, I might also add, has provided me with adequate remuneration as well as the privilege to teach in some of the most glorious natural locations in the world.

As to the word *prophet* itself, I decided to query Siri for her linguistic advice. Perfunctorily, she offered two definitions: "an inspired teacher" and a "visionary." Can I honestly claim my hard work was inspired enough to qualify me as some kind of a prophet?

I believe that most of my students, and many readers of my books, do consider me to be an "inspired teacher." And yes, I have pursued a compelling vision throughout my entire adult life! Further, like the legend of Johnny Appleseed, I planted the seeds of this vision wherever in the world those ideas might take root and grow. I feel deeply touched knowing I now have more than seventy international trainers carrying this healing work to forty-four countries. They have truly lightened my load and, in doing so, have given me the freedom to write this book, and to play more—with emphasis on play! It has been a wonderful journey, becoming an unsuspecting, and admittedly flawed, "quasi-prophet" in the healing of trauma. And the journey has not been a solitary one; lest I forget to mention, I had major help from so many friends and colleagues along the way and from my inner guidance.

During the weeks after my conversation with Efu, I continued to reflect on the depth of her words, and my lingering and seemingly inexhaustible self-doubt. I digested her challenge and began gradually, and hesitantly, to allow myself a guarded acceptance of this solemn mantle. The thought of being ridiculed for excessive hubris still frightened me. But even so, I've decided to wrestle with this word and what it means to me—and then to recover some of the uninhibited chutzpah, or courage, lost in a childhood of threat and fear. My family endured years of ongoing terror from death threats by the New York mafia. Any public visibility could be lethal. But one who travels the circuitous road from confining fear, terror, shame, and insecurity to the expansive realms of adventure, creativity, healing, and even inspiration becomes an emergent light in a tunnel of darkness.

12

Living My Dying

Dancing through the Eye of the Needle

Only a person with unlived lives is afraid to die. A person who feels he has lived his life—the way he wanted—is not afraid.

Norman O. Brown (quoted in
Kelemen's *Living Your Dying*)

In writing this final chapter, I find myself reflecting on whether this is the beginning of the end, or the end of the beginning; or perhaps both. It seems I am living my dying while reconnecting with that vital, enthusiastic two-year-old essence I still harbor. I contemplate the Latin roots of the word *enthusiasm*, which comes from "en-theos," meaning "with God." I yearn to connect more deeply with that child who walks with God, to play and dance with him and glory in his quicksilver, spontaneous joy in life and in death. And I ask, what does it mean to stare death in the face for the final act, not as I had earlier in my brushes with death, or my encounters with stillness and nothingness during trauma healings, but that ultimate face-off—the end of this life's journey?

Eros and Death

*Energy is the only life and is from the Body and Reason
is the bound or outward circumference of Energy. . . .
Energy is pure delight.*

WILLIAM BLAKE

Writing about Eros takes me, haltingly, to an encounter with my own mortality. As I completed the section on Eros, I wondered what comes next: What is the final chapter in my healing journey? But then I realized it was staring me in the face. This life's journey is about the welded unity of Eros and death. The orgasm has, for example, been compared to *une petite mort*, or a little death. This is an expression that originally meant "a brief loss or weakening of consciousness." In modern usage, however, it refers primarily to "the sensation of post-orgasm as likened to death." It is when we momentarily lose consciousness and drift off into an "ecstatic oblivion." Here, orgasm, *la petite mort*, is both a physical release and a spiritual opening.

The "blackout" of orgasm is but one expression of Eros. However, there are more gradual, gentler paths for expanded awareness. I have personally experienced how Eros can also involve a slow surrender, a powerful letting go, alongside a chosen other, into our deep sensations and feelings while still maintaining conscious awareness. This tantric-like practice allows us to feel our body while also maintaining a connection with our lover, a unity grounded in support, safety, and caring.

In the words of William Blake, "Energy is the only life and is from the Body," and, "Energy is pure delight." This conveys the essence of how it feels to be in a living, sensing, knowing body. For me this embodiment has been the task of a lifetime. A part of me protests that this is unfair—that just when I am moving toward becoming more fully in my body, I am readying to shed it in the final episode. But then, I reassure myself, this doesn't have to happen all at once—it can be a gradual transition, and I still have plenty of energy and vivacity to engage in life. I embrace this "opportunity of a lifetime" with openness and acceptance.

As an aside, I suspect one of the reasons why the use of psychedelics has become so popular is this: they also facilitate a surrender into the void, an "ego death," a relinquishing of control. As I mentioned in chapter 4, I do have some caveats and precautions regarding their use. However, whatever the catalyst, I believe this embrace of surrender is what it means to be living our dying.

Some years ago, I unexpectedly had my first taste of a "mini" death. I had been undergoing cataract surgery on both my eyes. It is a procedure done in intervals that are usually separated by two weeks. This protocol avoids cross infections and possible blindness. The night before the second operation, I had a dream: I was entering a large room where some kind of meditation retreat seemed to be taking place. As I walked into the room, there was a couple on the right, lying together in a large bed. I asked the teacher what they were doing, and he told me they were practicing the "death meditation." I eagerly declared that I wanted to do the same. To this bold pronouncement, he sternly but compassionately pointed to the left side of the room and instructed me to go there, where the beginners were practicing. My ego deflated like a punctured balloon. After I awoke from the dream, I realized I had to approach death with a beginner's mind.

The next day I was off to the surgery suite for the second eye procedure. I knew I wanted a more conscious encounter with the death experience, brought on by the anesthesia, for this second operation. So I made a request of the perplexed anesthesiologist. I asked him to count backward from three, and then, at zero, to administer the Propofol sedation. I clearly remember dissolving into a mini death, a peaceful surrender into nonexistence. Strangely I felt no fear. When I awoke in the recovery room, I felt clear and focused, and had no nausea or discomfort. I became very aware of my surroundings, which seemed unusually bright and clear, as though everything were vibrating.

For me this brief encounter with Propofol gave me the impetus to delve further into my death inquiry. I was painfully aware of a deeply rooted residual anxiety that kept me from fully settling in my body and thus knowing the joy of life energy coursing spontaneously through this living vessel of mine. If I was not fully alive and wholly inhabiting my sensing body, could I still face death? For this part of my healing journey, I turned to a very powerful catalyst, "Toad Medicine." This substance, 5-MeO-DMT, comes from a secretion of a particular gland of the Sonoran Desert Toad, or *Bufo alvarius.* It is likely one of the most powerful psychedelics. This catalyst has some similar effects to ayahuasca; however, it seems orders of magnitude more potent. In addition, the intense core experience lasts only about thirty to forty minutes. This brevity can be a benefit; although it is necessary to allow a few additional hours to quietly integrate such a powerful journey.*

Prior to using this medicine, I knew I wanted to choose a safe, contained setting and to have a clear intention. Since my core anxiety related to being alone and unsupported, and to my fear of death,

---

*Once again, I do not advise anyone to try such a powerful catalyst, or any psychedelic for that matter, without careful preparation, a qualified and psychologically minded guide, and adequate follow-up.

I was determined to find a resonant "shaman" and a truly supportive "midwife." I found such a midwife in a wonderful woman named Raina, a consummate healer and steady presence who offered to accompany me as I went under the effects of this powerful substance. I clarified to both my attendants that I wanted to face whatever inner demons might still be interfering with my wholeness, completion, and preparation for dying.

The moment I inhaled the substance, I seized Raina's hand as I dropped from sitting to lying down with a sleep mask covering my eyes. Initially I seemed to lose consciousness and fell into a nameless, speechless terror. It took me right to the place where I was stuck, to total disintegration and annihilation. But then, slowly, I made my way back from this land of the dead, this underworld of Hades, and found my route home. The warmth of Raina's hand and the subtle ambient soundscape allowed me to pace my return, as I wandered through a graveyard and wasteland of desiccated remains and fossilized ghosts. It was surely an "ego death"—and then, suddenly, the land opened up into verdant pastures, meandering streams, stately mountains, and deep, fertile valleys. I was moving forward in my quest to know death, to find a release from grabbing onto life and attachment.

I had first used this substance for excavating and facing my six-month-old abandonment terror. Now I set an intention to use it as a vehicle for encountering the oblivion of dying. And, in that death, I have found life renewed. Perhaps this is the universal and continuous cycle of "death and rebirth": through death, life renewed can emerge.

A sensible person might inquire, "Why in the world would I want to expose myself to such a disturbing ordeal, and moreover, to do so on multiple occasions?" The answer is not simple, nor is it particularly complex. I chose to take 5-MeO-DMT because in the past it has helped me return to a state of joy and grace; to the unwounded, vital, perennial part of my Self; to the essence of that lovely, innocent child. See plate 20. And during the few sessions I have undergone, there has been a clear progression forward, out of anxious disembodiment and toward inner wholeness and peace. My engaging of death has helped me open to the other side, to a renewed "joie de vivre" and enhanced life force. In death, as I have discovered, there is life, the universal cycle of death and rebirth, a life renewed and made accessible.

5-MeO-DMT has been called the God molecule; but it is certainly not all about love and light! Perhaps the American physicist Alfred Romer put it best when he wrote, "There has come to me an insight into the meaning of Darkness. The reason one must face his [or her] darkness, and enter into that darkness is not that he [or she] may return purified to face God. One must go into the darkness because *that is* where God is."[1] The Sufi poet Rumi said it in his inimical, cursive way: "Be grateful for whoever comes, because each has been sent as a guide from beyond."[2] I register these two writers' wisdom as a lodestar and guiding compass.

Though this part of my journey is incomplete, the steps I have taken give me hope that when death comes in its finality, I will be able to embrace it with less fear. Perhaps I will even welcome the absolute understanding that I am a speck of dust in this mysterious and continuous cycle of death and rebirth. But before this ultimate letting go, as my friends can attest, I still have much living to do on this physically embodied plane.

As I come to the end of our shared journey, I leave you to consider these chapters and avenues of healing that have been useful for me. I thank you for being my witnesses on this adventure, this exploration of the great mystery of life. So, dear reader, from my being to yours, I offer the hope that my healing journey may inspire you to visit and engage yours. I trust we all have our unique stories, our inner journeys to visit and to tell. I hope you will take the time to find your own voice.

There is a Hebrew saying, *Tikkun Olam*, which means to leave the world a better place than we found it. It is my hope that I will have left the world a better place, and that all of us can do the same. I am grateful for this opportunity to share my story with you. I close with a few words from a Navajo chant:

May you walk in beauty. . . .
May you stand tall in grace.

May you also tell your story.

Notes

Chapter One. Born into a World of Violence

1. James Hollis, *The Eden Project*, 16.

Chapter Two. Healing with Science and Shamanism

1. Rainer Maria Rilke, *Letters to a Young Poet*, 35.
2. Rebecca Frankel, "The Forgotten Jews of the Forest."
3. C. G. Jung, "Psychological Types," in *The Collected Works of C. G. Jung, Vol. 6*, 400.

Chapter Eight. Many Cultures, One Race: The Human Race

1. "Native Words, Native Warriors," chapter 5: "Coming Home," National Museum of the American Indian—Smithsonian website.
2. Aaron Levin, "The Long Journey Home," *American Indian* 21:3 (2020).
3. John Huston, *An Open Book*, 125.

Chapter Nine. The Four Most Important Women in My Life

1. Mira Rothenberg, *Children with Emerald Eyes*, 17.

2. Mira Rothenberg, *Children with Emerald Eyes*, 20.

3. Mira Rothenberg, *Children with Emerald Eyes*, 25.

4. Mira Rothenberg, *Children with Emerald Eyes*, 25.

5. Mira Rothenberg, *Children with Emerald Eyes*, 211.

6. Mira Rothenberg, *Children with Emerald Eyes*, 214–15.

7. Mira Rothenberg, *Children with Emerald Eyes*, 211–12.

8. Mira Rothenberg, *Children with Emerald Eyes*, 212.

9. Mira Rothenberg, *Children with Emerald Eyes*, 212.

10. Mira Rothenberg, *Children with Emerald Eyes*, 214.

11. Mira Rothenberg, *Children with Emerald Eyes*, 216.

12. *The Crown*, season 3, episode 1, "Olding," directed by Benjamin Caron, written by Peter Morgan, Jonathan Wilson, and Jon Brittain.

Chapter Ten. The Four Most Important Men in My Life

1. René Thom, *Structural Stability and Morphogenesis*, 325.

2. "Watson: Behaviorism," *Parenting and Family Diversity Issues*, Iowa State University Digital Press.

3. Nick Joyce and Cathy Faye, "Observation: Skinner Air Crib," *Association for Psychological Science*, website

Chapter Twelve. Living My Dying

1. Alfred Romer quoted in Philips, Howes, and Nixon, *The Choice Is Always Ours*, 82. Emphasis mine.

2. Jalaluddin Rumi, "The Guest House."

Bibliography

Degan, Raz, director. *The Last Shaman*. Abramorama, 2016. 1 hr., 17 min.

Einstein, Albert. *Relativity: The Special and General Theory*. New York: Henry Holt and Company, 1921.

Gibran, Kahlil. *The Prophet*. New York: Alfred A. Knopf, 1966.

Hollis, James. *The Eden Project: In Search of the Magical Other*. Toronto: Inner City Books, 1998.

Huston, John. *An Open Book*. Boston: Da Capo Press, 1994.

Jung, C. G. "Psychological Types," in *The Collected Works of C. G. Jung, Vol. 6*. Edited and translated by Gerhard Adler and R. F. C. Hull. Princeton: Princeton University Press, 1976.

———. "The Transcendent Function," in *The Collected Works of C. G. Jung, Vol. 8*. Edited and translated by Gerhard Adler and R. F. C. Hull. Princeton: Princeton University Press, 1976.

Philips, Dorothy Berkley, Elizabeth Boyden Howes, and Lucille L. Nixon, eds. *The Choice Is Always Ours: The Classic Anthology on the Spiritual Way*. Rindge, NH: Richard R. Smith, 1956.

Prigogine, Ilya. *An Introduction to Thermodynamics of Irreversible Processes*. New York: Interscience Publishers, 1961.

Rebecca Frankel, "The Forgotten Jews of the Forest," *New York Times*, September 4, 2021.

Rilke, Maria Rainer. *Letters to a Young Poet*. Translated by M. D. Herter Norton. New York: W. W. Norton and Company, 1962.

Rothenberg, Mira. *Children with Emerald Eyes: Histories of Extraordinary Boys & Girls*. Berkeley, CA: North Atlantic Books and Lyons, CO: The Ergos Institute, 2002.

Schrödinger, Erwin. *What Is Life?: With Mind and Matter & Autobiographical Sketches*. Cambridge, UK: Cambridge University Press, 2012.

Sinnett, A. P. *Esoteric Buddhism*. New York: Houghton, Mifflin, and Co., 1889.

Thom, René. *Structural Stability and Morphogenesis: An Outline of a General Theory of Models*. Translated by D. H. Fowler. Reading, MA: W. A. Benjamin, 1975.

Todd, Mabel E. *The Thinking Body: A Study of the Balancing Forces of Dynamic Man*. Highstown, NJ: Princeton Book Company, 1959.

van der Kolk, Bessel, M.D. *The Body Keeps the Score: Brain, Mind, and Body in the Healing of Trauma*. New York: Viking, 2014.

Vonnegut, Kurt. *Cat's Cradle*. New York: Dell Publishing Co., 1963.

Other Books
by Peter A. Levine

Waking the Tiger: Healing Trauma

Healing Trauma: A Pioneering Program for Restoring the Wisdom of Your Body

Sexual Healing: Transforming the Sacred Wound

In an Unspoken Voice: How the Body Releases Trauma and Restores Goodness

Trauma and Memory: Brain and Body in a Search for the Living Past; Understanding and Working with Traumatic Memory

With Maggie Klein, Ph.D.

Trauma-Proofing Your Kids: A Parents' Guide to Instilling Confidence, Joy and Resilience

Trauma Through a Child's Eyes: Awakening the Ordinary Miracle of Healing

With Maggie Phillips, Ph.D.

Freedom from Pain: Discover Your Body's Power to Overcome Physical Pain

About Somatic Experiencing (SE)

The Somatic Experiencing method is a naturalistic and neurobiological body-oriented approach to healing trauma and other stress disorders. The SE approach releases traumatic shock and restores connection, which is key to transforming PTSD and the wounds of emotional and early developmental attachment trauma. It offers a framework to assess where a person is "stuck" in the fight, flight, or freeze responses and provides clinical tools to resolve these fixated physiological states to restore the authentic self with self-regulation, relaxation, wholeness, and aliveness.

Human beings have an innate ability to overcome the effects of diverse traumas. The SE approach facilitates the completion of self-protective motoric responses and the release of thwarted survival energy bound in the body and nervous system, thus addressing the root cause of trauma symptoms. This is approached by gently guiding clients to develop increasing tolerance for difficult bodily sensations and suppressed emotions, building their capacity for containment and resilience.

Dr. Levine believes that the traumatic event isn't what causes long-lasting trauma, it is the overwhelming trapped response to the perceived life-threat that is causing an imbalanced nervous system. Somatic Experiencing's aim is to help one access the *body memory* (procedural memory) of the event, not the story. It is not necessary to share the details of your trauma history to do SE. The objective is to diffuse the power of the narrative and remap the body memory to regain aliveness and flow. In *In an Unspoken Voice*, he wrote that trauma is not just what happened to us, but rather what we hold inside in the absence of a present and empathetic other.

Like other somatic psychology approaches, Somatic Experiencing is a *body first* approach to dealing with the problematic (and often-times physical) symptoms of trauma. It helps individuals create new experiences in their bodies; ones that contradict those of tension and overwhelming helplessness. This means that healing isn't about reclaiming memories or changing our thoughts and beliefs about how we feel, it's about exploring the sensations that lie underneath our feelings and beliefs, as well as our habitual behavior patterns.

Somatic Experiencing training programs are designed to be accessible to psychologists, psychotherapists, psychoanalysts, psychiatrists, social workers, counselors, addiction treatment specialists, body workers, osteopaths, occupational therapists, physical therapists, medical doctors, nurses, acupuncturists, dentists, yoga teachers, meditation teachers, art therapists, equine therapists, life coaches, first responders, corrections officers, educators, clergy, spiritual advisors, and support providers for children and those with special needs.

Somatic Experiencing Practitioners (SEP) are devoted to bottom-up somatic-based processing as they begin their client's healing journey. They have backgrounds in a variety of different modalities/psychotherapies so you can find one that specializes in other treatments of interest, like CBT, psychiatry, craniosacral, bodywork, or equine therapy to name a few. SEPs who've taken our training integrate SE work into their other practices to create a well-rounded healing experience. To take the training you must be approved by presenting what other healing modalities you use in your practice.

Remember, no two SE Practitioners are the same, and our nervous systems are not all the same. We recommend that you experience a few and see whom you resonate with the best.

For more information, please visit:
www.somaticexperiencing.com
www.traumahealing.org